HAL LEONARD

SITAR METHOD
DELUXE EDITION

T0071247

BY JOSH FEINBERG

Speed • Pitch • Balance • Loop

To access audio & video visit:
www.halleonard.com/mylibrary

Enter Code
2840-2662-0467-2758

ISBN 978-1-4950-7638-1

HAL•LEONARD®

7777 W. BLUEMOUND RD. P.O. BOX 13819 MILWAUKEE, WI 53213

Visit Hal Leonard Online at
www.halleonard.com

🔊 AUDIO TRACK LIST

▶ VIDEO LIST

CONTENTS

▶ INTRODUCTION

Welcome to the *Hal Leonard Sitar Method*! This book and its accompanying audio tracks and video lessons will give you an introduction to the sitar and its technique, as well as the practice, theory, and history of the *raga* music of Northern India. I have written this book for beginning music students and those coming to the sitar with experience on other instruments.

The book also introduces the sargam system of notation, which is the modern standard for raga-based music. It may be different from the standard Western notation you may have seen, but it is the best way to give you a solid foundation in Indian music, and the technique of sitar. I encourage you to refer to the Glossary in the Appendix for help with the numerous Indian music terms you will encounter in this method.

RAGA

According to a Sanskrit saying, "That which colors the mind is known as a raga." Practically speaking, a raga (or *raag*) is based on a scale, usually having between five and twelve notes. A raga may have stressed/unstressed notes, phrases, and a general grammar of its own which help to bring forth a particular melodic character or mood. There are also *shrutis*, or microtones, which are used to evoke the proper feeling of a particular raga. In fact, there may be many different ragas based on the same scale. In this book, we won't be dealing with the nitty-gritty details of ragas (to do that, one needs to learn in person with a master), but we will be focusing on exercises and compositions in ragas which you can learn, practice, and perfect as a first step along your journey in raga music.

Raga music has its origins primarily in Northern India, but it is also practiced in Nepal, Bangladesh, Pakistan, and Afghanistan. Up until the early 20th century (prior to Indian independence), raga music was mostly played in courts for kings. Musicians were paid well and given quarters to live in with their families. The music was very tightly guarded; court musicians generally only taught their families and people the king requested them to teach. Students, sometimes called disciples, would usually live with their teacher, learning and practicing throughout the day entirely by ear (*aurally*) and memory. This sort of training would go on for years, often decades.

The preferred way for teachers to transfer music, and for students to pick it up, is still by ear. This way of learning, while being more labor intensive for both the teacher and the student, provides a much more thorough training for the student. Ear training, memory, improvisation, creativity, quick thinking, and ownership of the music are all skills which are developed and honed through the aural tradition, and are all crucial to good musicianship. Because raga music evolved aurally, the notational system is a fairly recent development, and is mainly used as an aid to memory.

Nowadays, teachers do not have kings and patrons supporting them, so they have to tour to earn a living. This is wonderful for spreading raga music to new listeners, however, it can make it difficult for a student to receive proper training. This method book is designed to get the student started, as well as provide material to those students who might not have a teacher living nearby. Do not rely solely on the notation in this book to learn new compositions and exercises—it can be difficult to know if you are playing it correctly without an audio reference. Read the book thoroughly and learn the notation, but also use the audio and video when you are learning new material. This will give you the best training possible in this type of learning environment.

ABOUT THE AUDIO & VIDEO

The accompanying audio contains demonstrations for most of the material in this book. You can use these recordings to help you tune, analyze the notation, and learn the examples.

 TRACK 1

The *tanpura* practice track is a recording of the drone sound that usually accompanies sitar; you can use it as a tuning reference, and put it on repeat to accompany your practice. There are also many rhythm practice tracks played by *tabla*, the pair of tuned drums which accompanies sitar. You can play with the tanpura and tabla practice tracks, but you should also use a metronome and get your own tabla/tanpura program so you can change the speed, rhythmic cycle, etc.

Some tracks include both sitar and tabla/tanpura accompaniment. When both are played together, the tabla and tanpura will be on the left channel and the sitar will be on the right. This will enable you to play along with the sitar while you are learning the composition, and then play it by yourself with just the accompaniment part. Play along with all the tracks to learn the material, and then practice it on your own. As you get more comfortable with a piece of music, increase your playing speed little by little.

This Deluxe Edition also includes exclusive video lessons taught by the author. Watch for the numbered video icons throughout the book.

To access the audio and video files, visit **www.halleonard.com/mylibrary** and enter the code found on page 1 of this book.

ABOUT THE AUTHOR

Josh Feinberg is a performer and educator of sitar and raga music based in Portland, Oregon. Josh received the bulk of his training from Ustad Ali Akbar Khan and his students, including Ustad Aashish Khan, Sri Alam Khan, and Sri Anindya Banerjee. He has a Bachelors degree in music from the New England Conservatory and is currently pursuing his MFA through Goddard Collage. Josh has also received guidance from Pt. Swapan Chaudhuri, Pt. Anindo Chatterjee, and Pt. Tejendra Majumdar. Though he is young, Josh is being lauded as one of the most promising sitarists of his generation. Josh maintains a busy touring and teaching schedule throughout the U.S., India, and Europe. He recently recorded his debut album *Homage* featuring Pt. Swapan Chaudhuri on tabla. Josh teaches at Lewis and Clark College and Reed College. For more information about Josh, and to purchase CDs or books, please visit his website at **www.joshfeinbergmusic.com**.

THE SITAR

The sitar is one of the most popular instruments to come out of the Indian subcontinent. There are three basic styles of the instrument, named after the musicians who popularized them: Ravi Shankar, Nikhil Banerjee, and Vilayat Khan. The Ravi Shankar and Nikhil Banerjee model sitars are very similar; both have four melody strings including two bass strings. However, Nikhil Banerjee uses three drone (or *chikari*) strings, while Ravi Shankar uses two. Instruments in both these styles usually include an upper gourd (or *toomba*) attached to the top of the neck.

The Vilayat Khan-style instrument differs greatly from the other two. Instruments in this style are slightly smaller. They have two melody strings (no bass strings), and four chikari strings. They are often decorated much more simply than the Ravi Shankar/Nikhil Banerjee-style instruments, and generally do not include an upper toomba.

FINDING AN INSTRUMENT

Finding a decent instrument can be difficult if you don't know what to look for. Purchasing second-hand can be risky if you're just starting out. It is best to purchase from a reputable dealer. The Ali Akbar College Store (**www.aacm.org**) is a good recommendation for students. They're the most established importer of Indian instruments in the U.S. They have a wide selection, and they do any required set-up work before shipping the instrument. A beginning student should get the cheapest instrument that is fully functional until they are ready to commit to a more costly instrument. The *Radha Krishna Sharma #3* is a good choice.

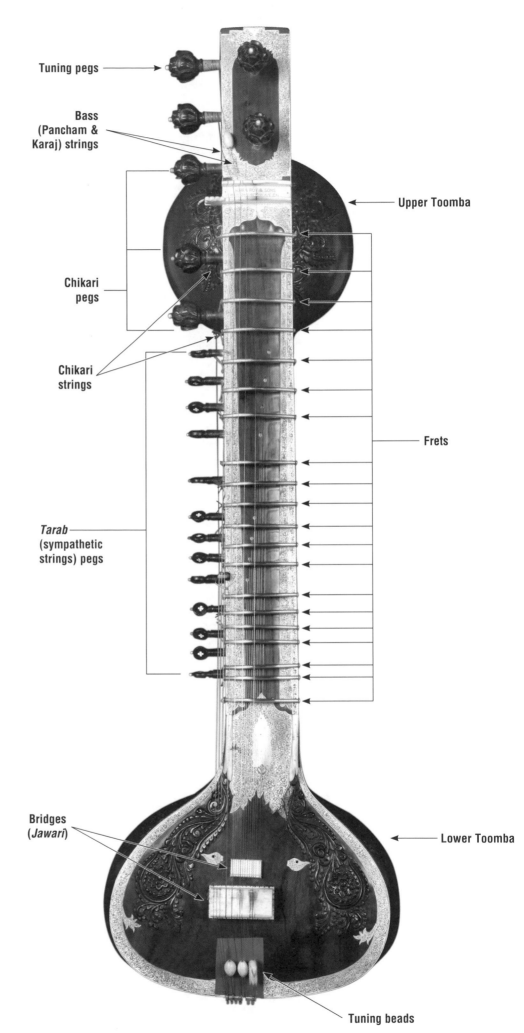

Tuning pegs

Bass (Pancham & Karaj) strings

Chikari pegs

Chikari strings

Tarab (sympathetic strings) pegs

Bridges (*Jawari*)

Upper Toomba

Frets

Lower Toomba

Tuning beads

SARGAM AND NOTATION

In order to know how to approach the sitar as an instrument, it is best to get to know some of the fundamentals of raga music and its notation first. Refer back to this section as needed while you progress through the book.

The name *sargam* is actually a contraction of the first four notes of the system: **Sa**, **Re**, **Ga**, and **Ma**. (**SaReGaMa** = **sargam**.) It is very important to learn the names of the notes, as this is our primary method for referring to the different pitches.

You might be familiar with *solfege* in Western music, which gives a syllable to each of the notes in a scale:

Do   Re   Mi   Fa   Sol   La   Ti   Do

Sargam begins with the same sort of concept, but expands it into an entire notational system, with several variations. The basic notes are (representing one *octave*, or eight notes):

Sa   Re   Ga   Ma   Pa   Dha   Ni   Sa
(Pronounce Re like "Ray," and Ni like "knee.")

When writing sargam, we use the first letter of each note:

S   R   G   M   P   D   N   S

The natural scale in North Indian music is called *Bilawal*. It is the same as the major scale in Western music. The position for the notes in this scale is called *shuddh* (pronounced the same as "should," since all the notes are in their natural, unaltered positions).

The Bilawal scale shows all the natural notes; nothing is sharp (*tivra*) or flat (*komal*). This scale looks like this:

S   R   G   m   P   D   N   S

Notice the "m" is the only note that is lowercase. **Ma** is the only note that is lowercase when shuddh, and it is also the only note that can be made tivra (sharp). The tivra **Ma** looks like this:

Tivra Ma: M

The notes **Re**, **Ga**, **Dha**, and **Ni** can be lowered by one half step.

Shuddh: R   G   D   N

Komal: r   g   d   n

Sa and **Pa** are immutable; they can never be made sharp or flat.

When notes are made komal or tivra for a particular raga (melody), they generally do not change for the whole performance of that piece. Therefore, we do not have to say shuddh, komal, or tivra, but simply the name of the note. There are many ragas that use more than one version of a note, such as both komal and shuddh **Ga**, however we still verbally refer to both the notes as **Ga**. We only use shuddh, komal, or tivra for instructional purposes.

SARGAM (NOTES)

On sitar, we tune our instrument to a key that sounds good, just like a singer might change the key of a song to suit his or her vocal range. Sitarists usually tune to the key of D or C♯. In a traditional sitar recital, the accompanying instruments (tabla and tanpura) will tune to the sitarist, so it is not necessary to tune to a "standard" pitch the way Western musicians do. Using a non-standard pitch is only a problem if you are playing with Western or tempered instruments, which have a standard pitch reference (A440). If you are playing with non-Indian instruments, it's usually best to use a tuner, piano, or other source to tune right at D or C♯.

We will be playing in the key of D for this book. We refer to this by saying that our **Sa** is D.

The Bilawal scale, or natural scale, now corresponds to the Western scale of D major:

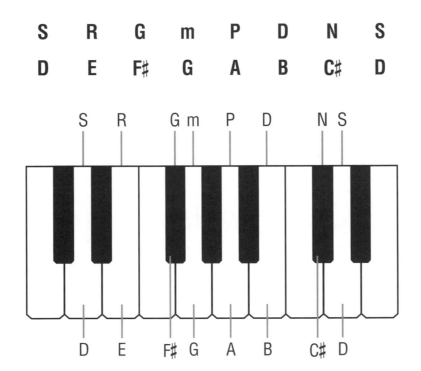

RHYTHMIC NOTATION

If a note is written by itself, it will have a value of one beat. (Depending on what method you use for counting, a beat can be one click of a metronome, one hand clap, or one foot tap. If you're counting "one, two, three, four," each number is a beat.) If the beat is divided into more than one note, it is notated by a *slur* underneath the notes (**S S**). One slur represents one beat; anything that is included in that slur occurs within that beat.

The chart below shows a **Sa** note repeated in various groupings within a beat. The same groupings are also shown in Western notation, for those who are familiar with it.

S = ♩ = 1 note per beat

S S = ♫ = 2 notes per beat

S S S =  = 3 notes per beat

S S S S =  = 4 notes per beat

S S S S S =  = 5 notes per beat

A *rest*, or pause between notes, is notated by a dash (–).

— = 𝄽 = 1 beat rest

S — = ♪ 𝄾 = 1 note for half the beat & a rest for the other half

— — — S = 𝄿 𝄿 𝄿 ♪ = 3 sixteenth rests, then 1 sixteenth note
(play the note at the end of the beat)

S — S — = ♩. ♩. = 2 notes, each lasting 1.5 beats (3 beats total)

S S S S — =  = 4 thirty-second notes, then 1 eighth rest
(Inner slur and dash for the rest are each half a beat. Inner slur
is divided into four equal parts, resulting in the four 32nd notes.)

When a rest comes *after* a note, we generally just let the note ring. The rest serves primarily to mark the duration of the note.

Bar lines show the groupings of the rhythmic cycle, just like in Western music. A cycle of four beats, one note per beat, would be shown like this:

$$\left| \quad S \quad S \quad S \quad S \quad \right|$$

Repeat signs tell you to repeat everything between the two signs.

$$\|: \quad S \quad S \quad S \quad S \quad :\|$$

Commas and *accents* denote phrasing and articulation.

S S S , S S S   The comma shows you how the phrasing should be played.

>
S   The accent above a note means that note should be played louder than others.

SPECIAL TECHNIQUES

Techniques such as *meend* (pulling) and *krintan* (hammer-ons, pull-offs, and sliding) are used liberally in sitar music. We will cover these techniques later on, but for now just use this section to become familiar with the notation.

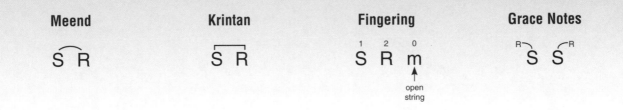

Meend	Krintan	Fingering	Grace Notes
S͡ R	S R	1 2 0 S R m ↑ open string	S S

REGISTER

This photo shows the general register (range) and orientation of the sitar neck as it relates to the pitches and frets. If a note is written just as a letter, it means that it is in the middle octave (eight-note interval) of the Ma string of the sitar. You'll learn more about the sitar's strings and notes in the next section; see page 16. If there is a dot below it, it means it is below middle **Sa** (fret 7 on the Ma string). If there is a dot above the letter, it means it is at high **Sa** or above it.

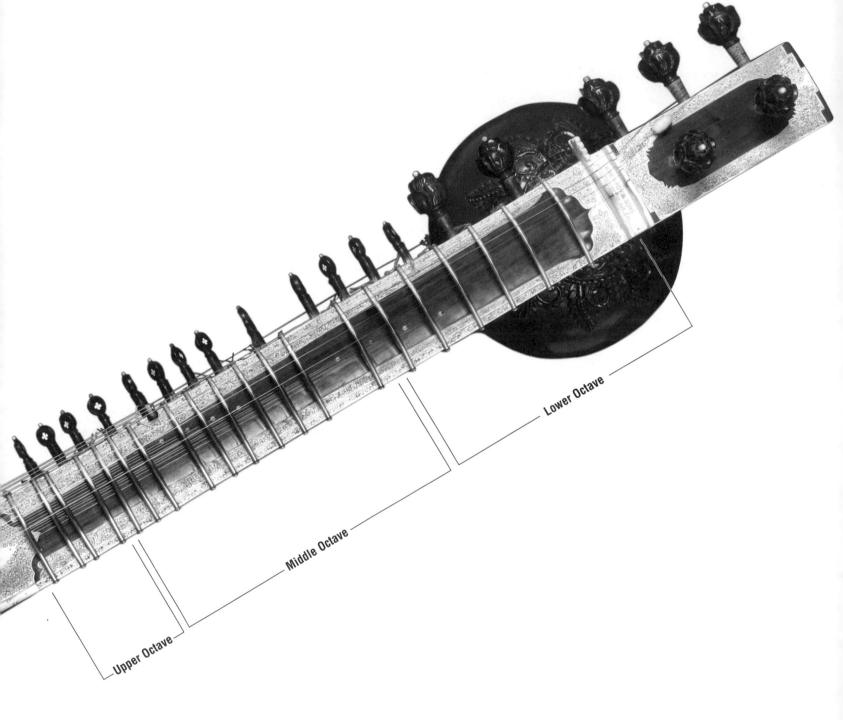

For example, these notes are below middle **Sa** (in the lower octave):

S R G M P D N

And these notes are in the higher octave:

S R G M P D N

VIDEO 2

TUNING

Now let's explore tuning the sitar. First, check to see if your sitar has bass strings (*pancham* and *karaj*—see the chart on page 7). If it does, make sure there is a hook on either the top fret, or screwed into the pick guard. This hook holds the bass strings out of the way while we are playing fast passages. The bass strings are not often played, and they can be very difficult to master. For now you should put the strings under the hook to avoid a sloppy, noisy sound while you are playing. If your instrument doesn't have a hook, you should remove those two strings. You can always put them on again later.

For the purposes of this book, we'll be tuning to D. The diagram on page 16 shows the notes that correspond to each tuning peg for all the open strings.

TARAB (SYMPATHETIC STRINGS)

It is important to tune the *tarab* (sympathetic strings) first. These strings ring "sympathetically" with the vibrations of the main strings. If they are out of tune, they may vibrate and disrupt the tuning of the other strings. To pluck the sympathetic strings for tuning, reach under the main strings from the top with your thumbnail, or from the bottom with your first or second finger.

 TRACK 1

Begin by playing the lowest (or longest) tarab string, and comparing it with the first note on the tanpura track, **Sa** (D). (If you have a piano, you can use the D note closest to middle C as a tuning source.) The peg for this string is the small peg right next to the big peg. (The big peg is the high **Sa** in the chikari strings.) Turn it until the string's note matches the audio (clockwise = lower; counterclockwise = higher). This might take a few tries at first. If you are using an electronic tuner, be sure to check the audio to make sure you are tuning to the correct register (or octave).

Now that the first sympathetic string is in tune, you can use a tuner to tune the rest of them relative to the first. Refer to the chart on page 16 for the note names.

MAIN AND CHIKARI STRINGS

Now that the sympathetic strings are tuned, we can move on to the Ma string, the first bronze Sa string, and the chikari strings in the same direction we've been moving (Pa, middle Sa, high Sa). Don't worry about the pancham and karaj strings for now (if your sitar has them)—they will remain tucked under their hook or off the sitar until you need them.

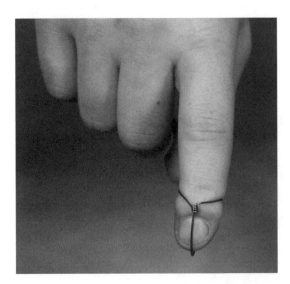

It's a good idea to put on the *mizrab* (finger pick) before tuning the main strings, since that's how we'll be playing them. Place it snugly (but not too tightly!) over your right-hand index finger as shown.

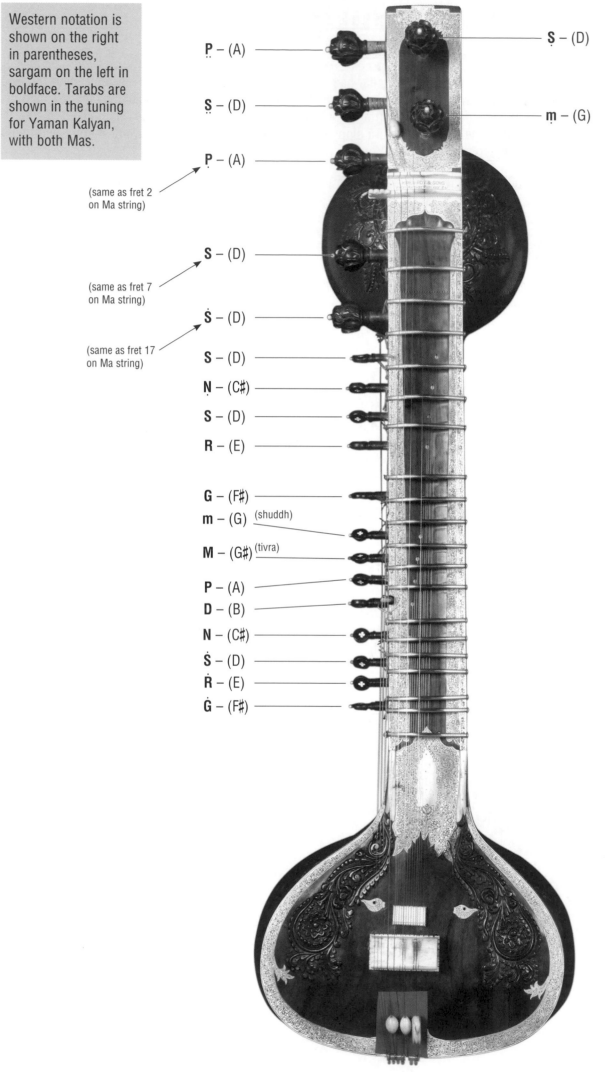

Western notation is shown on the right in parentheses, sargam on the left in boldface. Tarabs are shown in the tuning for Yaman Kalyan, with both Mas.

P̣ – (A)

Ṣ – (D)

P̣ – (A)

(same as fret 2 on Ma string)

S – (D)

(same as fret 7 on Ma string)

Ṡ – (D)

(same as fret 17 on Ma string)

S – (D)

Ṇ – (C♯)

S – (D)

R – (E)

G – (F♯)

m – (G) (shuddh)

M – (G♯) (tivra)

P – (A)

D – (B)

N – (C♯)

Ṡ – (D)

Ṙ – (E)

Ġ – (F♯)

Ṣ – (D)

m̤ – (G)

TUNING VARIATIONS

The chart on the facing page shows a standard way of tuning, but there are variations which are used for different ragas. The most common variations have the **Pa** in the drone strings (chikari) being tuned to **Ma** (as in the ragas *Rageshree*, *Bageshree*, and *Malkauns*). The tarab strings are always tuned to the raga you are playing. The names of the notes in the tarab strings remain the same, but the particular version of each note depends on the scale of the raga. For example, if a string is tuned to **Ga** (F♯) and you are playing raag *Madhuvanti*, which has komal (flat) **Ga**, then you should tune that string to komal **Ga** (F natural). The string is still tuned to **Ga**—that did not change—but we had to change it to the lowered **Ga** to adjust for the raga.

In some cases, a raga will have fewer than seven notes. When this happens, you may tune the unused note to either the next note up or the next note down. For example, in raga *Megh* there is no **Ga**. So, we can tune the "Ga" tarab string to either **Re** or **Ma**. The same is true for the **Dha** tarab string—we can tune it either to **Pa** or **Ni**. For each new raga that is introduced in this book, you will be shown the differences in tuning.

Here is a list of the tarab tunings for all the ragas in this book, starting at the lowest tarab string (the longest one).

Yaman Kalyan: S Ṇ S R G m M P D N Ṡ Ṙ Ġ

Madhuvanti: S Ṇ S R g M P P D N Ṡ Ṙ ġ

Megh: S ṇ S R m m P P n n Ṡ Ṙ ṁ

Khammaj: S Ṇ S R G m m P D n N Ṡ Ġ

TUNING PEGS AND BEADS

For all the tuning pegs along the side of the neck and the main Ma string, turning counterclockwise raises pitch and clockwise lowers the pitch. The only exception is the *Jor* string—the higher bronze Sa string—which will get higher clockwise and lower counterclockwise.

To keep the pegs tight, push them in while turning, like a screw. They should be tight enough not to slip, and no tighter. If it is an older sitar, the pegs can get polished by friction with the hole—you'll see a shiny band around the peg where it meets the hole. To fix this, take 220 grit sandpaper and lightly rough up the peg. Then apply a light coating of wax-free chalk (like sidewalk chalk) to the peg where it meets the sitar.

The fine-tuning beads should be taken to a slack position before playing, and then pushed very slightly down so they do not rattle. Tune the string with the peg and get it as close as possible before using the beads for fine tuning.

MOVING FRETS

The frets on a sitar are tied on using silk or nylon thread. This was the primary method of attaching frets to instruments before inlaid frets were developed. An advantage of using these types of frets is that we can adjust them for very precise intonation. However, they may move from time to time, so checking them often for good intonation is a must. You can do this by ear, or use an electronic tuner.

The sitar is not chromatically fretted; in other words, there isn't a fret for every note—there are some gaps. There is only one **Re** fret and one **Dha** fret in the middle octave. In the upper octave, there is only one **Re**, **Ga**, and **Ma** fret. This means that you may have to move some frets if you play a raga that uses one of the notes that is omitted, such as komal **Re** (flat **Re**, or E♭).

For now, adjust your fret position according to this chart. It shows the notes that should sound at each fret when played on the Ma string.

> Note: The high **Ga** fret (fret 19) is shown here in the komal position. You will need this fret to be in the shuddh position for Yaman Kalyan, the first raga in this book. Likewise, fret 20 should be in the tivra, or raised position, for Yaman Kalyan.

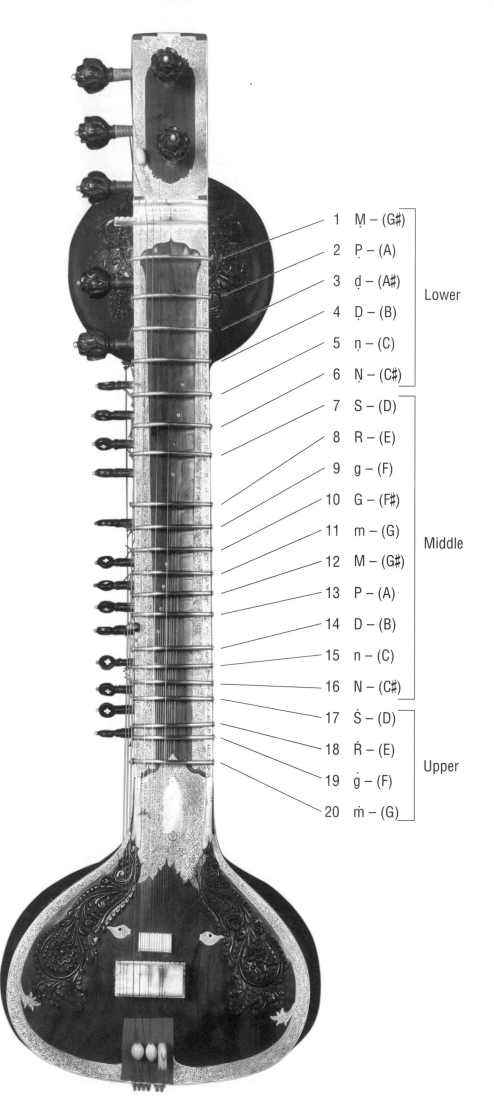

1	Ṃ – (G♯)	Lower
2	P̣ – (A)	
3	ḍ – (A♯)	
4	Ḍ – (B)	
5	ṇ – (C)	
6	Ṇ – (C♯)	
7	S – (D)	Middle
8	R – (E)	
9	g – (F)	
10	G – (F♯)	
11	m – (G)	
12	M – (G♯)	
13	P – (A)	
14	D – (B)	
15	n – (C)	
16	N – (C♯)	
17	Ṡ – (D)	Upper
18	Ṙ – (E)	
19	ġ – (F)	
20	ṁ – (G)	

To check the fret position, start at the bottom, and pressing the Ma string with your index finger to the left of the fret, pluck the string. Adjust the fret as shown to change the pitch.

To move a fret, first lay your sitar on the floor. Grasp both ends of the fret in one hand and pull it in the desired direction. (To lower the pitch, move the fret away from the main gourd; to make it higher, move it toward the main gourd.) Use your other hand to pull the thread on the back of the neck while you pull the fret. Check the intonation by first making sure the open Ma string is in tune, then playing it at the fret you just moved. Continue making fine adjustments to the fret position until you are confident it is in tune.

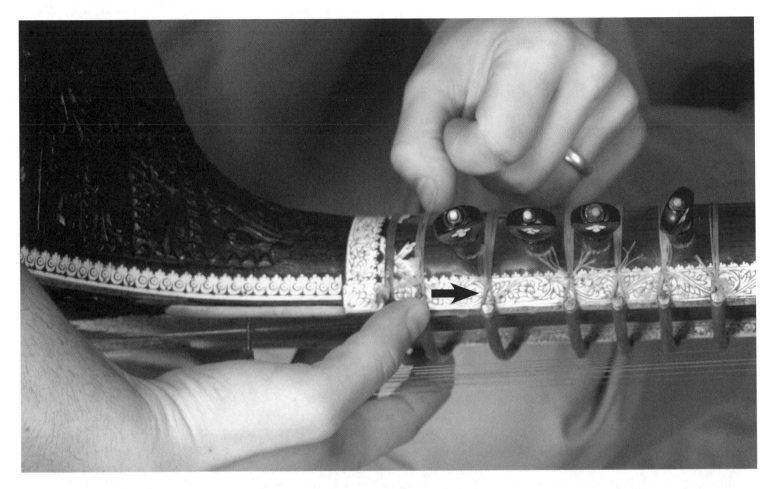

RECOMMENDED LISTENING

Listening is one of the most important aspects of learning how to play music. Listening will get your ear and mind ready to absorb material and help you pick up the "accent" of the music. A serious student should be listening to sitar, or raga music, at least several times a week. There are too many great musicians to list, so here are some recommendations to start with:

- Nikhil Banerjee (sitar)

- Vilayat Khan (sitar)

- Ravi Shankar (sitar)

- Rais Khan (sitar)

- Shahid Parvez (sitar)

- Ali Akbar Khan (sarod)

- Aashish Khan (sarod)

- Alam Khan (sarod)

- Tejendra Narayan Majumdar (sarod)

◉ HOLDING THE SITAR

One of the most intriguing aspects of the sitar, especially to the audience, is how we hold the instrument. Indian music is generally performed sitting on the floor (preferably on a nice clean rug), and the playing position of the sitar has evolved to fit that tradition.

These instructions are oriented for right-handed sitar players. If you are playing a left-handed instrument, reverse the directions and use the hand or foot opposite to the ones mentioned. Please keep in mind that this playing position involves some flexibility for you to be comfortable in it. If you cannot sit cross-legged comfortably, it can take several months of stretching to be able to hold the sitar properly. If you are having trouble holding the sitar in the traditional posture, try using one of the alternate playing postures discussed in this chapter until you are able to sit more comfortably with the instrument. You should endeavor to sit with the gourd on your foot, in the traditional posture, as this offers the greatest control and safety for the instrument.

TRADITIONAL POSTURE

Sit cross-legged on the floor, left foot under your right leg. The sitar should be on its back, strings facing the ceiling, on the floor in front of you. The lower toomba (gourd) of the sitar should be on your right side, and the neck will be on the left. Take your left foot and slide it further under your right leg until it sticks out a little. Now pick up the sitar, rotate it so the strings are facing away from your chest, and the wooden face of the sitar is perpendicular to the ground. Place the gourd of the sitar in the arch of your left foot. Now it's time to place your arm on the sitar. Take your right arm, and lay it over the top of the gourd.

Try to hold the sitar using the right arm and the foot the gourd is resting on. We don't want the left hand to hold the sitar at all—we need that hand to remain free to move up and down the neck. To do this, you must use leverage between your right arm and left foot and the neck must be at the proper angle. The neck should be at a 45-degree angle to the ground or higher. The higher you hold the neck, the easier it will be to avoid using your left hand. This will take some practice, but with a little effort, you can master it.

ALTERNATE POSTURES

If you use one of these alternate postures, don't rely on it forever—use it only until you are able to hold the sitar properly. The alternate postures involve putting the gourd on the floor, and over time this can cause it to crack. Make sure you are sitting on a rug. You may even want to put the gourd of your sitar on a small pillow (as pictured) rather than having it rest directly on the floor.

Alternate Posture #1

Sit on the floor cross-legged (it doesn't matter which leg is on top), and rest the gourd on the floor to the right of your right leg. Use the same arm positions as described in the "traditional posture" section.

Alternate Posture #2

Kneel on the floor, and then sit back onto your feet. Now move your hips to the right so you are sitting on the ground and both your legs are folded to the left of you. Follow the right-hand positions shown in the "traditional posture" section.

RIGHT HAND POSITION

With your right arm over the top of the gourd, your thumb should rest on the top of the neck of the sitar at the last fret. A good way to check your arm position is to make sure the first knuckle on the index finger of your right hand (the one closest to your hand) is directly over the chikari strings.

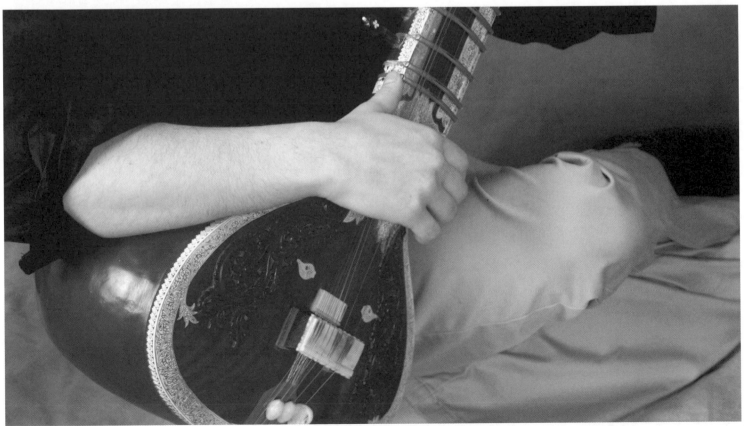

LEFT HAND POSITION

The left hand should be placed on the sitar with the thumb behind the neck and the index and middle finger on the Ma string (the bottom steel string).

When we fret a note with the index finger, the thumb should be directly behind it on the back of the neck. When we fret a note using the middle finger, the thumb should be either behind the index finger, or in between the index and middle fingers.

Try to avoid rolling the sitar back towards you so you can see your fingers on the string. Instead, use your thumb on the fret thread on the back of the neck as a reference. (Since the thumb will be behind the index finger, you will be able to feel the thread that ties that fret to the neck.) Rolling the instrument towards you makes playing much more difficult—your left hand will have to wrap around the neck further, and your right hand will be at an awkward angle to the strings. Try to keep the face of the sitar perpendicular to the ground while playing.

LEFT HAND TECHNIQUE

In the beginning, we primarily use the index finger (labeled as 1) to play up and down the neck. We use the middle finger (labeled 2) to pull the string and for techniques such as krintan (hammer-on/pull-off). The ring finger (also labeled 2) is used to substitute for the middle finger when the reach is too big, or when you get tired. Try not to pull the string using this finger. The pinky is generally not used, except for a few special and advanced techniques, which we won't be covering in this book.

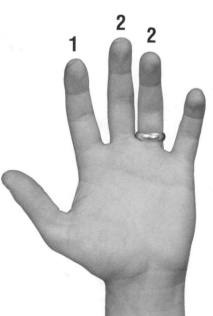

BOLS
VIDEO 4
(RIGHT HAND STROKES)

The first right-hand stroke we will be learning is called *Da*, an upward stroke on the Ma string. This is the dominant stroke in sitar playing. Keeping your thumb on the neck, close your hand as if you are making a fist (except without moving your thumb). The motion should come from the wrist, not just the fingers. Even though we are only using the index finger to actually pluck the string, we want the whole hand, all the fingers, to move with the index finger. This is where our strength, power, and speed will come from.

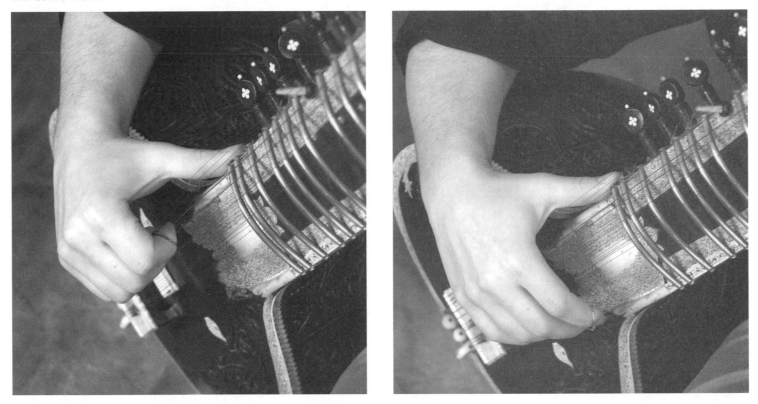

The next stroke is called *Ra*; it is a downward stroke on the Ma string. For those of you coming from a guitar playing background, it might be tempting to play Ra as the dominant stroke. This is a habit you must break. On sitar, Ra is primarily used in fast lines by alternating between Da and Ra (up and down), though there are many different applications for it in more advanced techniques. The hand should move from the wrist when playing Da and Ra, not just the fingers. It should be very similar to when you let your hand hang in front of you limp, and then make a fist—the wrist will automatically come up.

The next stroke is called *Diri*. This is simply Da–Ra played quickly. Diri is usually twice as fast as Da and Ra played separately. In Western notational terms, you can think of Da and Ra as quarter notes, and Diri as eighth notes.

The last stroke is called *Chik*, which is a downward stroke on the chikari strings (the three steel drone strings on the top part of the neck). These strings are always played at the same time; they are not played one at a time except when tuning the instrument. Sitars can have two, three, or four chikari strings, but the technique for playing them is the same. Hold your right index finger above the chikari strings, and in one quick motion, play a downstroke, striking all the chikari strings at once.

Bol Notation:

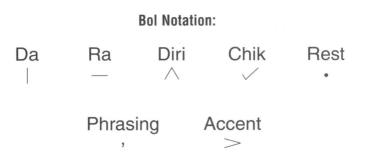

Bol notation symbols are usually written below the note names in sargam notation. For the following exercises, we will show the bol notation by itself.

BOL EXERCISES

First, play these exercises on the open Ma string. As you become familiar with scales, play them twice for each note of a scale. Start on the low **Pa**, and go to the highest fret on your sitar (usually **Ma**, although sometimes **Ga**). Try not to add any gaps that are not listed in the exercises. If you need more time, it's best to play the notes evenly at a slow speed, rather than adding a pause between the notes.

When playing any right-hand strokes, you should strike both the Ma string and the Sa (Jor string). This will help promote a fully extended stroke. There are other types of strokes, including one in which we only play the Ma string, but in the beginning let's focus on the two-string stroke to help build your right hand technique.

Bols for Strokes 1–8 ▶ VIDEO 4 1:58

1. |

2. | —

3. | — |

4. | — | —

Count: 1   2   3   1   2   1   2   1   2   3
5. | — | , | —   *or* | — , | — |

Count: 1   2   1   2   1   2   1   2   3   1   2   3
6. | — , | — , | —   *or* | — | , | — |

Count: 1   2   1   2   1   2   3
7. | — , | — , | — |

or 1   2   1   2   3   1   2
     | — , | — | , | —

or 1   2   3   1   2   1   2
     | — | , | — , | —

8. | — | — | — | —

or 1   2   3   1   2   3   1   2
     | — | , | — | , | —

or 1   2   3   1   2   1   2   3
     | — | , | — , | — |

or 1   2   1   2   3   1   2   3
     | — , | — | , | — |

Patterns with Four Beats VIDEO 5

1.
	Da	Da	Da	Da
Count:	1	2	3	4
	│	│	│	│

2.
	Diri	Diri	Diri	Diri
Count:	1 +	2 +	3 +	4 +
	∧	∧	∧	∧

3.
	Da	Diri	Diri	Diri
Count:	1	2 +	3 +	4 +
	│	∧	∧	∧

4.
	Da	Ra	Da	Diri
Count:	1	2	3	4 +
	│	—	│	∧

5.
	Da	Diri	Da	Ra
Count:	1	2 +	3	4
	│	∧	│	—

6.
	Da	Ra	Diri	Diri
Count:	1	2	3 +	4 +
	│	—	∧	∧

Patterns of Three VIDEO 6

This is a more challenging bol because it has two Da strokes in rapid succession. This is a fundamental stroke, and it's very important to master it. First play it with a Chik to get the strokes in the proper direction, then take out the Chik and remove the gap.

1.
	Da	Ra	Da	Chik
Count:	1	2	3	4

2.
	Da	Ra	Da	etc.		
Count:	1	2	3	1	2	3

3.
	Da	Ra	Da	Da	Ra	Da	Da	Ra
Count:	1	2	3	1	2	3	1	2

The following pattern of three notes has a gap (or rest) on the second beat. It is a very important rhythm in sitar music; make sure you give the rest its full value.

Da		Ra	Da		Ra	etc.
1	(2)	3	1	(2)	3	(2 is silent)

Exercises Using This Bol VIDEO 6 2:15

1.
	Da		Ra	Da		Ra	Da	one stroke held for two counts
Count:	1	2	3	1	2	3	1 2	

2.
	Da		Ra	Da		Ra	Da	Ra
Count:	1	2	3	1	2	3	1	2

3.
	Da	Diri	Diri	Diri	Da		Ra	Da		Ra	Da
Count:	1	2+	3+	4+	5	+	6	+	7	+	8+

4.
	Diri	Diri	Da		Ra	Da		Ra
Count:	1+	2+	3	+	4	+	5	+

24

▶ PALTA AND MURCHHANA
(MELODIC PATTERNS)

Palta (pronounced *pol* from "pollinate" and *ta* from "pasta") are melodic patterns that we can use when we compose or improvise. These patterns are then moved starting on each note of the scale. (In Western music this is a called a *tonal sequence*.) Specifically, paltas are patterns which span less than one octave. There are nearly unlimited combinations that we can make.

Murchhana (pronounced *moor-chah-na*) is a pattern of notes that spans one octave. For example, playing a scale from **Sa** to **Sa** could be considered murchhana. Then we would take that pattern, and play it from all the other notes in the scale—**Re** to **Re**, **Ga** to **Ga**, etc. This is a very simple murchhana, but the patterns can get very complex as well.

The following patterns are written in the scale for *Yaman Kalyan*, a raga that will be taught in detail later in this book. The scale we use for Yaman Kalyan is called *Kalyan Thaat*. (Thaat is pronounced like "tot" from tater tot.) Kalyan Thaat is equivalent to the Western Lydian mode.

 TRACK 2

S   R   G   M   P   D   N   Ṡ

(D   E   F♯   G♯   A   B   C♯   D)

Play the following exercises starting on each note of the scale. The first two iterations of the pattern are shown; you should continue repeating them from each note in the scale until you reach the top of the sitar. There will be a slash (/) after the first two ascending patterns, then you will see the first two iterations of the pattern descending from the top. Again, play the pattern starting from each note in the scale until you reach the bottom register. The audio includes the pattern for the first few iterations up and down for demonstration purposes. You should continue the pattern on each note of the scale.

First, practice these patterns starting from the low **Pa** (fret 2) on the Ma string, to the highest fret on your sitar. This is usually a **Ma** fret (fret 20). Once you are comfortable with that, practice the pattern starting on the low Sa (the open second string) to the highest fret on your Ma string. This involves crossing strings and is therefore more challenging.

As you learn more scales and ragas, you can transfer these patterns into the scale of whatever raga you are learning. Make sure you use the appropriate notes (shuddh, komal, or tivra), and make sure you use only the notes present in the raga. (For the purposes of exercises, you do not have to follow the ascending/descending order of the raga; just use the scale.)

PRACTICE TIP

Before you try to play any of the following patterns, you should learn the scale you are going to use thoroughly, with no wrong notes.

When you are first learning these patterns, play them slowly. Once you are able to play it somewhat, practice with either a metronome or tabla machine. I recommend the iPhone/iPad app "iTabla Pro" for both tanpura and tabla accompaniment. It is the least expensive and best-sounding practice aid I have found.

EXERCISES

Two-Note Paltas

🔊 TRACK 3   ▶ VIDEO 7
1:08

Finger: 1   2   1   2   2   1   2   1

1. Ṗ Ṅ , Ḋ S , / Ġ Ṡ , Ṙ N

Bol: | | | | | | | |

2.   2   1   2   1   1   2   1   2

    Ḋ Ṗ , Ṅ Ḋ / Ṙ Ġ , Ṡ Ṙ

| | | | | | | |

PRACTICE TIP

Play with all Da (upstrokes) first, then switch to Da Ra for all patterns.

The second finger is used at the top of a pattern to change direction and go down. This is similar to the way a swimmer kicks off the wall in a turn. We generally do not slide up or down the neck with the second finger.

Three-Note Paltas

🔊 TRACK 4   ▶ VIDEO 8

3.   1 1 2   1 1 2   2 1 1   2 1 1

    Ṗ Ḋ Ṅ , Ḋ Ṅ S / Ġ Ṙ Ṡ , Ṙ Ṡ N

first: | | | | | | | | | | | |
then: | — | | — | | — | | — |

3a.   2 1 1   2 1 1   1 1 2   1 1 2

     Ṅ Ḋ Ṗ , S Ṅ Ḋ / Ṡ Ṙ Ġ , N Ṡ Ṙ

| — | | — | | — | | — |

4.   1 2 1   1 2 1   1 1 2   1 1 2

    Ṗ Ḋ Ṗ , Ḋ Ṅ Ḋ / Ġ Ṙ Ġ , Ṙ Ṡ Ṙ

| — | | — | | — | | — |

4a.   2 1 1   2 1 1   1 2 1   1 2 1

     Ḋ Ṗ Ḋ , Ṅ Ḋ Ṅ / Ṙ Ġ Ṙ , Ṡ Ṙ Ṡ

| — | | — | | — | | — |

Four-Note Paltas

🔊 TRACK 5   ▶ VIDEO 9

5.
   ¹P ¹Ḍ ¹Ṇ ²S , ¹Ḍ ¹Ṇ ¹S ²R / ²Ġ ¹Ṙ ¹Ṡ ¹N , ²Ṙ ¹Ṡ ¹N ¹D

| — | —   *etc.*

5a.
  ¹P ¹Ḍ ²N ¹P , ¹Ḍ ¹Ṇ ²S ¹Ḍ / ²Ġ ¹Ṙ ¹Ṡ ²Ġ , ¹Ṙ ¹Ṡ ¹N ²Ṙ

| — | —   *etc.*

5b.
  ¹Ḍ ²N ¹P ¹Ḍ , ¹Ṇ ²S ¹Ḍ ¹Ṇ / ²Ṙ ¹Ṡ ²Ġ ¹Ṙ , ¹Ṡ ¹N ²Ṙ ¹Ṡ

| — | —   *etc.*

5c.
  ²Ṇ ¹P ¹Ḍ ¹Ṇ , ²S ¹Ḍ ¹Ṇ ¹S / ¹Ṡ ²Ġ ¹Ṙ ¹Ṡ , ¹N ²Ṙ ¹Ṡ ¹N

| — | —   *etc.*

🔊 TRACK 6   ▶ VIDEO 9 5:14

6.
  ¹P ²Ḍ ¹P ²Ṇ , ¹Ḍ ²Ṇ ¹Ḍ ²S / ²Ġ ¹Ṙ ²Ġ ¹Ṡ , ²Ṙ ¹Ṡ ²Ṙ ¹N

| — | —   *etc.*

7.
  ¹P ¹Ḍ ²S ¹Ṇ , ¹Ḍ ¹Ṇ ²R ¹S / ²Ġ ¹Ṙ ¹N ¹Ṡ , ²Ṙ ¹Ṡ ¹D ¹N

| — | —   *etc.*

8.
  ¹P ¹P ²Ḍ ¹P , ¹Ḍ ¹Ḍ ²Ṇ ¹Ḍ / ²Ġ ²Ġ ¹Ṙ ²Ġ , ¹Ṙ ¹Ṙ ²Ṡ ¹Ṙ

| — | —   *etc.*

Five-Note Paltas

TRACK 7 VIDEO 10

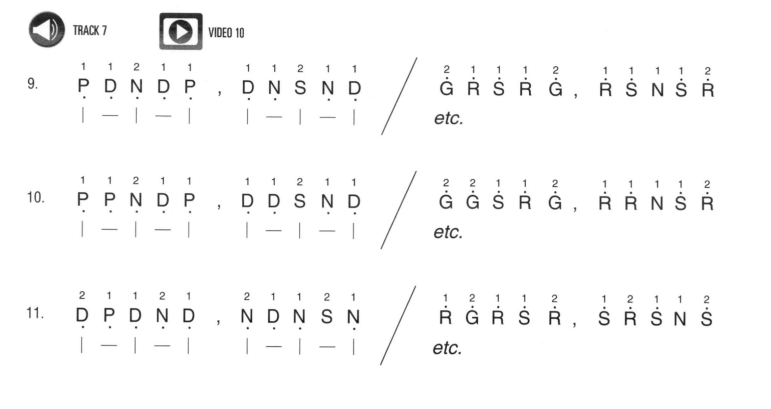

9.
```
   1 1 2 1 1       1 1 2 1 1        2 1 1 1 2     1 1 1 1 2
   P D N D P  ,  D N S N D     Ġ Ṙ Ṡ Ṙ Ġ , Ṙ Ṡ N Ṡ Ṙ
   | — | — |      | — | — |         etc.
```

10.
```
   1 1 2 1 1       1 1 2 1 1        2 2 1 1 2     1 1 1 1 2
   P P N D P  ,  D D S N D     Ġ Ġ Ṡ Ṙ Ġ , Ṙ Ṙ N Ṡ Ṙ
   | — | — |      | — | — |         etc.
```

11.
```
   2 1 1 2 1       2 1 1 2 1        1 2 1 1 2     1 2 1 1 2
   D P D N D  ,  N D N S N     Ṙ Ġ Ṙ Ṡ Ṙ , Ṡ Ṙ Ṡ N Ṡ
   | — | — |      | — | — |         etc.
```

Six-Note Paltas

TRACK 8 VIDEO 11

12.
```
   1 2 1 1 1 2       1 2 1 1 1 2        2 1 2 1 1 1     2 1 2 1 1 1
   P D P D N S  ,  D N D N S R     Ġ Ṙ Ġ Ṙ Ṡ N , Ṙ Ṡ Ṙ Ṡ N D
   | — | — | —         etc.
```

13.
```
   1 1 2 2 1 1       1 1 2 2 1 1        2 1 1 1 1 2     1 1 1 1 1 2
   P D N N D P  ,  D N S S N D     Ġ Ṙ Ṡ Ṡ Ṙ Ġ , Ṙ Ṡ N N Ṡ Ṙ
   | — | — | —         etc.
   or | — | | — |        etc.
```

TRACK 9 VIDEO 11 3:05

14.
```
   2 1 1 1 2 1       2 1 1 1 2 1        1 1 2 1 1 2     1 1 2 1 1 2
   N D P D N D  ,  S N D N S N     Ṡ Ṙ Ġ Ṙ Ṡ Ṙ , N Ṡ Ṙ Ṡ N Ṡ
   | — | — | —         etc.
   or | — | | — |        etc.
```

15.
```
   1 1 2 1 2 2       1 1 2 1 2 2        2 2 1 2 1 1     2 2 1 2 1 1
   P P D P N N  ,  D D N D S S     Ġ Ġ Ṙ Ġ Ṡ Ṡ , Ṙ Ṙ Ṡ Ṙ N N
```

Seven-Note Paltas

TRACK 10 VIDEO 12

```
    1   2   1   2   1   1   2      1   2   1   2   1   1   2
16. P   D   P   D   P   D   N  ,   D   N   D   N   D   N   S        /
    .                             
    |  —  |  —  |  —  |          |  —  |  —  |  —  |
```

```
    2   1   2   1   2   1   1      2   1   2   1   2   1   1
    G   R   G   R   G   R   S  ,   R   S   R   S   R   S   N
    .   .   .   .   .   .   .      .   .   .   .   .   .
    |  —  |  —  |  —  |          |  —  |  —  |  —  |
```

Experiment with different bols and groupings.

VIDEO 12
1:39

```
    1   1   2   1   2   1   1      1   1   2   1   2   1   1
17. P   D   N   D   N   D   P  ,   D   N   S   N   S   N   D        /
    .   .   .   .   .   .   .      .   .   .   .   .   .
    |  —  |  —  |  —  |          |  —  |  —  |  —  |
```

```
    2   1   1   2   1   1   2      1   1   1   2   1   1   2
    G   R   S   R   S   R   G  ,   R   S   N   S   N   S   R
    .   .   .   .   .   .   .      .   .   .   .   .   .
    |  —  |  —  |  —  |          |  —  |  —  |  —  |
```

```
    1   2   2   1   2   1   1      1   2   2   1   2   1   1
18. P   N   N   D   N   D   P  ,   D   S   S   N   S   N   D        /
    .   .   .   .   .   .   .      .   .   .   .   .   .
    |  —  |  |  —  |  —          |  —  |  |  —  |  —      /
```

```
    2   1   1   2   1   1   2      1   1   1   2   1   1   2
    G   S   S   R   S   R   G  ,   R   N   N   S   N   S   R
    .   .   .   .   .   .   .      .   .   .   .   .   .
    |  —  |  |  —  |  —          |  —  |  |  —  |  —
```

A WORD ON FINGERING

Generally speaking, we only use the index (1) and middle (2) finger on the left hand to fret notes. However, we can use the ring finger to substitute for the middle finger if the stretch is too far. If a finger is marked 2, but you are having trouble reaching the note comfortably, you can use your ring finger. Only use the third finger to substitute for the second. We don't play fingers 123 in succession as it is a weak hand position for pulling; you can hurt yourself doing that.

Eight-Note Paltas

19.
```
 1  1  2    1  1  2    1  1    1  1  2    1  1  2    1  1
 P  D  N ,  D  N  S ,  N  D ,  D  N  S ,  N  S  R ,  S  N     /
 |  —  |    |  —  |    |  —    |  —  |    |  —  |    |  —
```

```
 2  1  1    2  1  1    1  2    2  1  1    2  1  1    1  2
 G  R  S ,  R  S  N ,  S  R ,  R  S  N ,  S  N  D ,  N  S
 |  —  |    |  —  |    |  —    |  —  |    |  —  |    |  —
```

20.
```
 1  2  1  2  1  2  2  2      1  2  1  2  1  2  2  2
 P  D  P  D  P  N  N  N  ,   D  N  D  N  D  S  S  S     /
 |  —  |  —  |  —  |  —         etc.
```

```
 2  1  2  1  2  1  1  1      2  1  2  1  2  1  1  1
 G  R  G  R  G  S  S  S  ,   R  S  R  S  R  N  N  N
```

21.
```
 1  2  1  2  1  2  1  2      1  2  1  2  1  2  1  2
 P  D  P  N  D  S  N  S  ,   D  N  D  S  N  R  S  R     /
 |  —  |  —  |  —  |  —         etc.
```

```
 2  1  2  1  2  1  2  1      2  1  2  1  2  1  2  1
 G  R  G  S  R  N  S  N  ,   R  S  R  N  S  D  N  D
```

22.
```
 2  1  1  1  2  1  2  1      2  1  1  1  2  1  2  1
 N  D  P  D  N  D  S  N  ,   S  N  D  N  S  N  R  S     /
 |  —  |  —  |  —  |  —         etc.
```

```
 1  1  2  1  1  2  1  2      1  1  2  1  1  2  1  2
 S  R  G  R  S  R  N  S  ,   N  S  R  S  N  S  D  N
```

PRACTICE TIP

Once you can play these patterns comfortably, experiment with accenting different notes in the pattern. You can try accenting different upstrokes or downstrokes for a different effect. It's amazing how an accent can make a simple palta sound much more interesting!

Murchhana

Play all these murchhana exercises first with all Da strokes, and then alternating Da-Ra.

TRACK 12   VIDEO 14

1.
1	1	1	1	1	1	1	2		1	1	1	1	1	1	1	2
P	Ḍ	Ṇ	S	R	G	M	P	,	Ḍ	Ṇ	S	R	G	M	P	D

first: (| | | | | | | |
then: (| — | — | — | —)

2	1	1	1	1	1	1	1		2	1	1	1	1	1	1	1
Ġ	Ṙ	Ṡ	N	D	P	M	G	,	Ṙ	Ṡ	N	D	P	M	G	R

2.
1	2	1	1	1	1	1	1		1	2	1	1	1	1	1	1
P̣	P	M	G	R	S	Ṇ	Ḍ	,	Ḍ	D	P	M	G	R	S	Ṇ

2	1	1	1	1	1	1	2		2	1	1	1	1	1	1	2
Ġ	G	M	P	D	N	Ṡ	Ṙ	,	Ṙ	R	G	M	P	D	N	Ṡ

3.
1	1	1	1	1	1	1	2	2	1	1	1	1	1	1	1
P	Ḍ	Ṇ	S	R	G	M	P	P	M	G	R	S	Ṇ	Ḍ	P̣	,

1							2								
Ḍ	Ṇ	S	R	G	M	P	D	D	P	M	G	R	S	Ṇ	Ḍ

2	1	1	1	1	1	1	1	1	1	1	1	1	1	2
Ġ	Ṙ	Ṡ	N	D	P	M	G	G	M	P	D	N	Ṡ	Ṙ	Ġ	,

1														2
Ṙ	Ṡ	N	D	P	M	G	R	R	G	M	P	D	N	Ṡ	Ṙ

4.
1	2	1	2	1	2	1	2	1	2	1	2	1	2	1
P̣	D	P̣	N	P̣	S	P̣	R	P̣	G	P̣	M	P̣	P	P̣	✓ ,

etc.

D	N	Ḍ	S	Ḍ	R	Ḍ	G	Ḍ	M	Ḍ	P	Ḍ	D	Ḍ	✓

2	1	2	1	2	1	2	1	2	1	2	1	2	1	2
Ġ	Ṙ	Ġ	Ṡ	Ġ	N	Ġ	D	Ġ	P	Ġ	M	Ġ	G	Ġ	✓ ,

etc.

Ṙ	S	Ṙ	N	Ṙ	D	Ṙ	P	Ṙ	M	Ṙ	G	Ṙ	R	Ṙ	✓

A BRIEF WORD ON FORM

ALAP

Form in raga music is fairly fixed: slow to fast, simple to complex. There are many, many sections in a performance and they must be played in order, however, sections can be omitted. Generally speaking, a performance will start with a *rubato* (free time) sitar solo called *Alap*. This is where the musician introduces the raga one note or one phrase at a time, and shows variations and ornaments on key phrases in a relaxed and unfixed rhythm. The Alap starts at middle **Sa**, then goes to the lower octave, and finally goes up to the higher octave.

JOR

Jor is similar to Alap, except now there is a steady pulse. There is still no set meter (number of beats) and no tabla. The Jor builds in the same fashion as the Alap: low to high, one note or one phrase at a time. The musician will also start playing faster and faster material using techniques such as *gamak*, *tans*, krintan, etc.

JHALLA

The next section is called *Jhalla*. Jhalla is characterized by fast right hand strokes, but slow melodies. You can think of it as a sort of high-energy tremolo, but there is also a lot of rhythm and groove happening. The standard patterns for Jhalla are Da Chik Chik Chik and Chik Da Da Da. These are played at a comfortable speed at first, but the musician will speed up over a few minutes until they reach their absolute top speed before ending.

GAT

Everything I just described is called *Alap-Jor-Jhalla*, or sometimes Alap for short. It may be as short as one minute, or more than an hour long. Once the tabla comes in, we have started a section called *Gat*. A Gat (pronounced like "gut") is a fixed instrumental composition accompanied by tabla. (It functions like the "head" in a jazz tune.) It is set to a particular *taal* (rhythmic cycle), which is usually from six to seventeen beats in length, played at a variety of speeds. The musician will improvise, returning to the Gat as a refrain when they are done developing a section. The tabla player may also take a turn at improvising a solo, while the sitarist repeats the Gat to mark the taal.

In a full presentation of a raga, a slow and fast Gat will be played. (In shorter pieces, it is not uncommon to play just one Gat and move on to another raga.) The fast Gat may speed up and include another section of Jhalla, this time with tabla. The faster sections are almost always played in *Tintal* (sixteen beats). This section may include *Saath Sangat* (sitar and tabla soloing at the same time and then coming back to beat 1 together), *Sawal Jawab* (a "question-and-answer" section), and other types of interplay with the tabla player. The raga is usually finished by playing either a *Tihai* (a phrase that repeats three times and lands on beat 1) or *Chakradar* (the same as a Tihai, but it repeats nine times).

Form for Playing a Gat (including the compositions in this book)

Gats generally start before *Sam* (pronounced like "sum"; beat 1 of the rhythmic cycle). For example, if you are playing a Gat which is set to a rhythmic cycle of sixteen beats (Tintal), the Gat may start on beat 9. That first line of the Gat from beat 9 to beat 1 (as in "9, 10, 11, 12, 13, 14, 15, 16, Sam") is called the *Mukhra*. That is the hook of the composition; we end our improvisations by leading them back to this phrase. When we play the Gat, **we are only allowed to stop on Sam; we cannot stop in the middle of the rhythmic cycle**. So, if our Gat starts on beat 9, we will play the first full line of the Gat which will bring us back to beat 9 again, and then play the Mukhra from beat 9, to Sam a second time, to lead us back to beat 1. This is the form for playing all Gats. Some Gats have more than one line. In that case, we always end by coming back to the first line and ending on Sam. The most important thing to remember is that we can only stop playing a Gat at the Sam in the first line of the Gat.

YAMAN KALYAN

Yaman Kalyan is arguably the most popular raga in this system of music. It is an evening raga, usually performed after sundown until about 11:00 pm. Yaman Kalyan is traditionally the first raga a student is taught. There is also raga *Yaman*, which, like Yaman Kalyan, has a very prominent tivra **Ma**. The difference between the two ragas is a slight use of the shuddh **Ma** in one phrase in Yaman Kalyan. Straight Yaman does not use the shuddh **Ma** at all.

TARAB TUNING

Begin by tuning the tarab strings to the raga. In this case, the string that was shuddh **Ma** (G) becomes tivra **Ma** (G♯), and what was tivra **Ma** becomes **Pa** (A). If you have less than thirteen sympathetic strings, then you can avoid doubling notes (i.e., having two strings tuned to **Pa**.)

S N S R G M P P D N Ṡ Ṙ Ġ
(D C♯ D E F♯ G♯ A A B C♯ D E F♯)

SCALE

We have already discussed the scale we use for Yaman Kalyan: Kalyan Thaat. Here it is again for review.

Kalyan Thaat

🔊 TRACK 2

Fret:	7	8	10	12	13	14	16	17
	S	**R**	**G**	**M**	**P**	**D**	**N**	**Ṡ**
	(D	E	F♯	G♯	A	B	C♯	D)

Play this scale up and down the Ma string using all Da strokes (upstrokes). Play Da four times on each note. Make sure you play both the Ma string and the lower Sa (Jor) string for every stroke.

P̣ Ḍ Ṇ S R G M P D N Ṡ Ṙ Ġ

 etc.

Ġ Ṙ Ṡ N D P M G R S Ṇ Ḍ P̣

EXERCISES

Now play the following exercises for this scale. (You may have seen some of these in the Bol or Palta section of exercises.) Only the first and second iteration of the pattern in either direction are written out. Just repeat the pattern on all the notes of the scale up and down.

Finger: 1   1   2   1   1   2   2   1   1   2   1   1

1.   P D N ✓ , D N S ✓ etc. / Ġ Ṙ Ṡ ✓ , Ṙ Ṡ N ✓ etc.

2.   P D N S , D N S R / Ġ Ṙ Ṡ N , Ṙ Ṡ N D

Try exercises 3 and 4 first with all Da strokes, then alternating Da-Ra.

3.   P D P N D N , D N D S N S / Ġ Ṙ Ġ Ṡ Ṙ Ṡ , Ṙ Ṡ Ṙ N Ṡ N

4.   P D P N , D N D S / Ġ Ṙ Ġ Ṡ , Ṙ Ṡ Ṙ N

5.   P D N S R G M P , D N S R G M P D / etc.

     Ġ Ṙ Ṡ N D P M G , Ṙ Ṡ N D P M G R

Now play each pair of notes with a Diri stroke. This should sound twice as fast as when you just play them with Da. In Western terminology, Da should sound like a quarter note and Diri should sound like two eighth notes. Make sure they are even, both with regard to rhythm and volume!

6.   P P P P P P P P , D D D D D D D D /

     Ġ Ġ Ġ Ġ Ġ Ġ Ġ Ġ , Ṙ Ṙ Ṙ Ṙ Ṙ Ṙ Ṙ Ṙ

34

ASCENDING AND DESCENDING SCALES

Ragas often have different scales—one for ascending and another for descending. In Yaman Kalyan, we skip **Sa** and **Pa** when we go up, and use all the notes when we go down.

Aroha (ascending):

N̤ R G M D N Ṡ

Avaroha (descending):

Ṡ N D P M G R S

Vadi (most important note): **Ga**

Samvadi (second most important note): **Ni**

CHALAN

Ragas often have certain notes which are emphasized, other notes which are not, and twists and turns in their movement. A *chalan* (pronounced chah-lahn) is a learning composition which gives the student a sort of roadmap for the raga. Memorize this and it will help you learn the next composition much more easily. Play everything first with Da strokes, then Da-Ra.

N̤ R G M	P M G R	G M D N	Ṡ N D P

M D N Ṙ	Ġ Ṙ Ṡ N	D P M G	R S N̤ R	G —

TINTAL

The following Gat (an instrumental composition which is accompanied by tabla) is set to Tintal, a rhythmic cycle of sixteen beats, grouped 4+4+4+4. The strokes the tabla plays for a rhythmic cycle are called *theka* (pronounced "take-ah").

TRACK 13   VIDEO 15

Theka for Tintal

	Sam								Kali							
	1	2	3	4	5	6	7	8	9	10	11	12	13	14	15	16
	Dha	Dhin	Dhin	Dha	Dha	Dhin	Dhin	Dha	Dha	Tin	Tin	Na	Na	Dhin	Dhin	Dha

Tabla is actually two drums: a high-pitched tuned drum on the right, and a bass drum on the left. *Na* is a stroke played on the rim of the high drum. *Tin* is a stroke played on the inner ring of the high drum. *Ge* is a resonant stroke played on the bass drum. When Na and Ge are played at the same time, we get *Dha*. When Tin and Ge are played at the same time, we get *Dhin*. Notice, then, that up to beat 9, the bass drum is playing every beat, but then drops out until beat 14. We call this *Kali*, which means "black" or "empty." By listening to where the bass drum drops out, we can find where we are in the cycle.

In every cycle, beat 1 is called Sam (pronounced like "sum"). This is the most important beat. It is the starting and ending point. Sam is notated with a plus sign (+), and Kali (the mid-point) is notated with a "0."

Before you learn this gat on sitar, listen to the audio and speak the theka for Tintal along with the recording.

COMPOSITION IN MEDIUM-FAST TINTAL

Gat

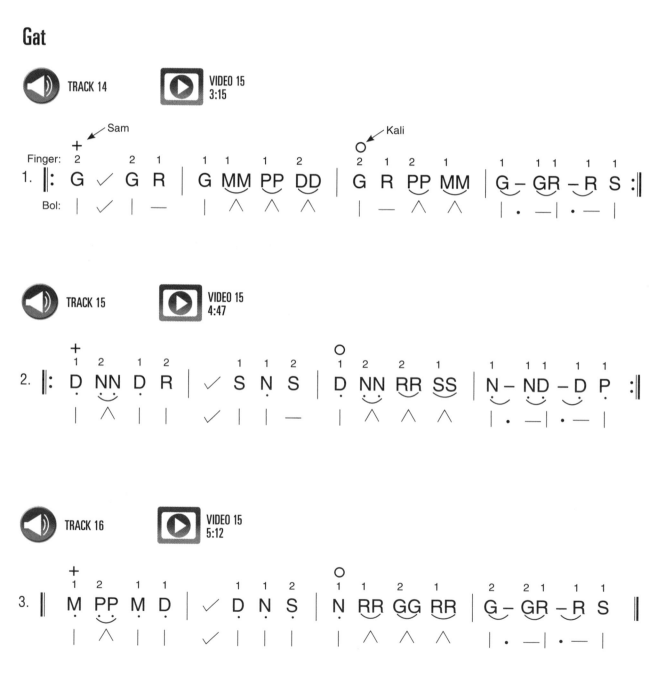

TANS

A *tan* (Tah-n) is a fast line. Tans are almost always played with Da-Ra or Diri bols. All of these tans have a starting beat above the first note—make sure you start in the correct place. For instance, the first example starts at Kali (beat 9), notated as 0, but the tabla on track 17 will start on Sam (beat 1). Listen to the count-ins on the track for a reference. After every tan, immediately start playing the first line of the Gat. In this way, the Gat functions as a sort of refrain, or chorus. Memorize these tans, play them slowly and cleanly, and then speed them up. For reference, a professional sitarist will play tans in a composition such as this from 180 beats per minute (bpm) to 350 bpm.

Note: Use the second finger when 2 is marked. If there is no marking, use the first finger.

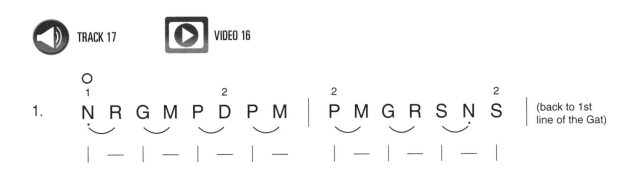

The tabla on track 18 will start on Sam; you should start this line on beat 5. Also, sometimes it is advantageous to shift or slide with the second finger, and here is one of those occasions.

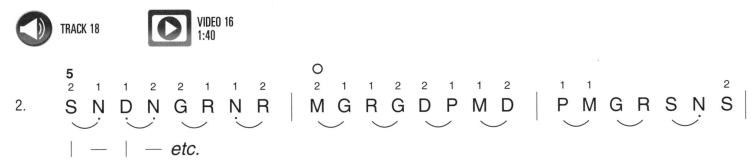

The tabla will start from Kali (beat 9); you should start this line from Sam (beat 1).

The tabla will start from Kali (beat 9); you should start this line from Sam (beat 1).

TRACK 20   VIDEO 17

+
2   1   2   1   2   1
4. ‖: G G G R | G M P ✓ | N R R G G R R |
     | | | | | | | | ∧ ∧ ∧

1   2   +
                                   2   1   2
G — G m — m G R | G — G S — N S :‖
| • — | • — | — | • — | • — |

O
2
Ṡ N D P M G R S | N R S N D P M P
| — | — | — | — | — | — | — | —

+
          2 2   1 2 2
P P M G R S | N N Ġ Ṙ Ṡ N
| | | — | — | | | — | —

O   +
D P M G R S N R | G N R G N R | (G)
| — | — | — | — | | — | | — |

38

MADHUVANTI

VIDEO 18

Raag Madhuvanti (Mah-doo-vahn-tee) is usually performed in the late afternoon or evening. Many people believe it to be borrowed from Carnatic (South Indian classical) music. Madhuvanti uses komal (flat) **Ga**, and tivra (sharp) **Ma**, so you will need to move the **Ga** and **Ma** fret in the higher octave to the appropriate position. Refer to the section on moving frets if you're unsure how to do this.

TARAB TUNING

Compared to Yaman Kalyan, Madhuvanti uses komal (flat) **Ga**. Tune both **Ga** tarab strings down from shuddh **Ga** (F♯) to komal **Ga** (F♮).

S Ṇ S R g M P P D N Ṡ Ṙ ġ

SCALE

S R g M P D N Ṡ

D E F G♯ A B C♯ D

EXERCISES

Play the following exercises in this scale. After you work through these, you can play any other exercise in this book in this scale. To save space, just the first and second iteration of the pattern in either direction are written out. Just repeat the pattern on all the notes of the scale up and down.

Finger: 1
1. Ṗ Ḍ Ṇ S R g M P D N Ṡ Ṙ ġ ġ Ṙ Ṡ N D P M g R S Ṇ Ḍ Ṗ
   | | | | *etc.*

     1 2   1 2   2 1   2 1
2. Ṗ N N , Ḍ S S / ġ Ṡ Ṡ , Ṙ N N
   | ∧ | ∧ | ∧ | ∧

3.

```
1 1 1 2 2 1 1        1 1 1 2 2 1 1
P D D N N D D   ,    D N N S S N N        /
| ^   ^   ^     |    ^   ^   ^

2 1 1 1 1 2 2        2 1 1 1 1 2 2
g R R S S R R   ,    R S S N N S S
| ^   ^   ^     |    ^   ^   ^
```

4.

```
2 1 1 1 2 1          2 1 1 1 2 1
N D P D N D   ,      S N D N S N          /
| — | — | —          etc.

1 1 2 1 1 2          1 1 2 1 1 2
S R g R S R   ,      N S R S N S
```

5.

```
1 1 2     1 1 2
P D N , D N S            /     g R S , R S N
| — |     | — |               etc.
                              2 1 1   2 1 1
```

40

ASCENDING AND DESCENDING SCALES

Aroha:

Ṇ S g M P N Ṡ

Avaroha:

Ṡ N D P M g R S

Vadi (most important note): **Pa**

Samvadi (second most important note): **Sa**

SARGAM COMPOSITION IN TINTAL

A *Sargam composition* is basically a simple Gat. They are usually used as learning tools, though they can be played in performance. The following composition is set to the rhythmic cycle of Tintal, sixteen beats. Refer to the section on Yaman Kalyan to review the cycle, if necessary.

Gat

TRACK 21

VIDEO 18
1:14

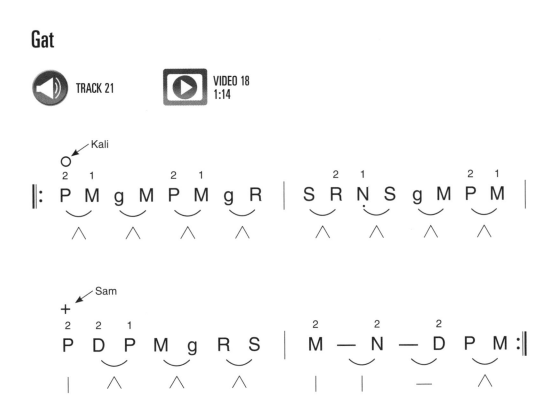

Tans

TRACK 22

VIDEO 18
2:21

TRACK 23

VIDEO 18
3:37

TRACK 24

VIDEO 18
4:15

MEEND

Meend (bending notes by pulling the string) is very important in sitar playing. Raga music uses "rounded" or "curved" notes, and meend is our primary way of obtaining that sound. Do not over-emphasize the slide between notes. Simply by virtue of the fact that we are pulling the string, there *will* be a slide, but our primary focus here is on playing the notes correctly in tune, and correctly in time. Slower slides get into issues of shruti (microtones) and *andolan* (very specific vibrato). This is a very complex area, and we won't be delving into it in this book.

We can do meend on the Ma string, the low Pancham string, and the Karaj string. On the Jor string, we can pull a maximum of a half step (e.g., from Ga to shuddh Ma). It is possible to pull more, but if you pull the Jor string more than a half step, it may break!

For now, we will only pull using both the first and second finger together for strength. When the frets start getting too small for you to put both fingers in one fret, just put the index finger on the fret immediately below the note you're playing (it doesn't have to be in the scale, because the second finger will fret the note that will sound).

MEEND TIPS

Meend can be very challenging. First, play the following meend exercises slowly and without a specific tempo, starting on each note up and down the scale. This will allow you to focus exclusively on pitch before moving on to timing. Once you are fairly comfortable, practice the same exercises slowly in time with tabla playing Tintal (track 13)—or you can use a metronome. Speed is not important at this point; we want to focus on clarity. After you can play these exercises in tune and in time, speed them up little by little.

Pay close attention to where the pluck falls. This will dramatically affect the articulation and phrasing of a pattern. We can create a variation of a pattern by changing where the pluck comes. First play the exercises as written, then experiment!

EXERCISES

The following exercises are in the scale of Yaman Kalyan. First practice them in Yaman Kalyan, then play them in the scale of whatever raga you are studying.

Two-Note Pulls

For the first exercise, pluck, pull, and pluck the bent string again.

TRACK 25

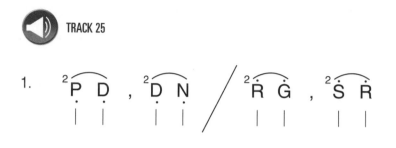

The next exercise starts with a pulled note; pluck the bent string, release it, and pluck again.

Now pluck once, bend, and let ring without plucking again.

Pluck the pre-bent string and release.

Three-Note Pulls

TRACK 26   VIDEO 19

5.   ²P D N ✓ , ²D N S ✓ / ²S Ṙ Ġ ✓ , ²N Ṡ Ṙ ✓

6.   ²N D P ✓ , ²S N D ✓ / ²G Ṙ Ṡ ✓ , ²Ṙ Ṡ N ✓

7.   ²P D P , ²D N D / ²Ṙ Ġ Ṙ , ²Ṡ Ṙ Ṡ

TRACK 27   VIDEO 20

8.   ²P D N N D P , ²D N S S N D / ²Ṡ Ṙ Ġ Ġ Ṙ Ṡ , ²N Ṡ Ṙ Ṙ Ṡ N

Four-Note Pulls

VIDEO 20
2:05

9.   ²P D N S S N D P , ²D N S R R S N D / ²N Ṡ Ṙ Ġ Ġ Ṙ Ṡ N , ²D N Ṡ Ṙ Ṙ Ṡ N D

Five-Note Pulls

VIDEO 20
4:24

We can pull five notes on each fret above **Pa**.

10.   ²D N S R G , ²N S R G M / ²D N Ṡ Ṙ Ġ , ²P D N Ṡ Ṙ

45

MEGH

Megh literally means "cloud." It is part of the *Malhar* group of melodies, which is associated with the monsoon in India. We can play Malhar ragas anytime during the rainy season. Some of them can also be played outside of the rainy season at night, however, Megh should only be performed during the monsoon.

If you are playing this raga coming from Madhuvanti, you will have to move your high **Ma** fret from the tivra (sharp) position back to shuddh (natural). If your sitar does not have a high **Ma** fret, you can move the high **Ga** fret to **Ma**. If you do not think you can get the intonation right by ear, use a tuner: **Ma** = G.

TARAB TUNING

S ṇ S R m m P P n n Ṡ Ṙ ṁ

SCALE

Megh is a *pentatonic* raga, meaning it has five notes. First play the entire scale as written below:

🔊 TRACK 28

S R m P n Ṡ Ṡ n P m R S

ASCENDING AND DESCENDING SCALES

Now play the pentatonic raga Megh in its ascending and descending forms:

Aroha:

ṇ S R m P n Ṡ

Avaroha:

Ṡ n P m R S

Vadi: Pa

Samvadi: Re

Important phrases: m͡R , R͡P , n͡P

PLAYING ON THE JOR STRING

Now let's introduce the idea of playing notes on the Jor string. The fretting of this string uses the same technique as the Ma string. **Re** on the Jor string is the 2nd fret. Here is an exercise to get you started crossing between the Jor and Ma strings. When you pluck the Jor string, try not to hit the Ma string. This will take some practice to master.

String:	Jor ------- Ma-- Jor-------l
Finger:	0 1 0 1 1 1 1 1 1 1 1 1 1 1 2 2 1 1 1 1 1 1 1 1 1 1 1 0 1 0

S R m P n S S R m P n S S R m m R S S n P m R S S n P m R S

Bol: | | | | *etc.*

EXERCISES

The first two exercises start on the Jor string.

TRACK 28 (cont.)   VIDEO 21

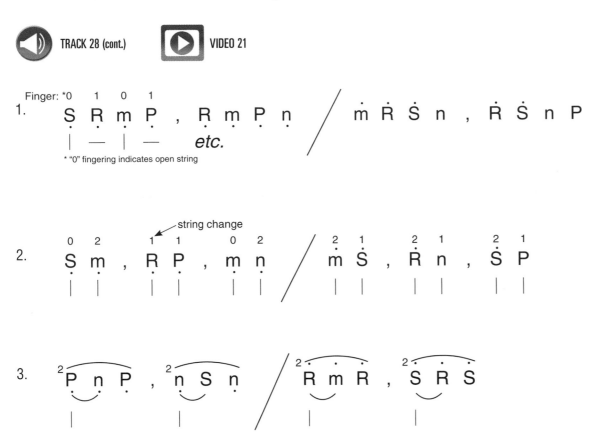

Finger: *0   1   0   1

1. S Ṛ m P , Ṛ m Ṗ ṇ / ṁ Ṙ Ṡ n , Ṙ Ṡ n P
| — | —   *etc.*

* "0" fingering indicates open string

string change

0   2   1   1   0   2   2   1   2   1   2   1

2. S m , Ṛ P , m ṇ / m Ṡ , Ṙ n , Ṡ P

3. ²⌢P n P , ²⌢n S n / ²⌢Ṙ m Ṙ , ²⌢Ṡ Ṙ Ṡ

The small note is a *grace note*—a short note without a rhythmic value of its own that usually accents another note.

VIDEO 21
4:28

4. ²ₙ⌢Ṗ , ²ₛ⌢n / ²ₘ⌢Ṙ , ²ᵣ⌢Ṡ

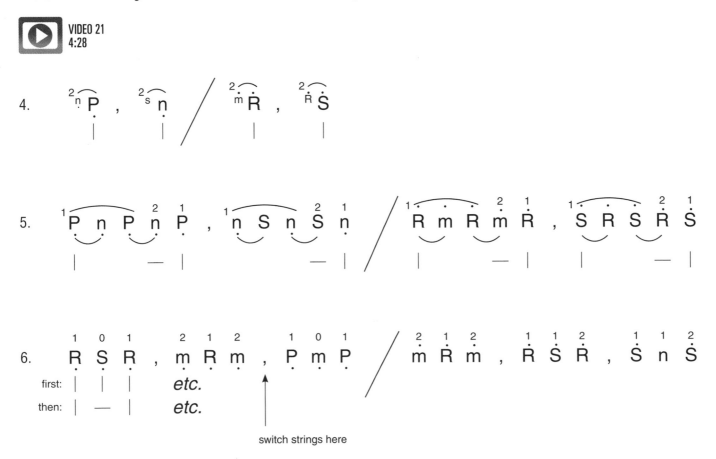

5. ¹⌢P n P ²n P , ¹⌢n S n ²S n / ¹⌢Ṙ m Ṙ ²m Ṙ , ¹⌢Ṡ Ṙ Ṡ ²Ṙ Ṡ

6. R Ṡ Ṛ , m Ṛ m , Ṗ m Ṗ / m Ṙ m , Ṙ Ṡ Ṙ , Ṡ n Ṡ

first: | | | *etc.*
then: | — | *etc.*

switch strings here

JHAPTAL

The following composition is set to a rhythmic cycle of ten beats called *Jhaptal*. It is grouped 2+3+2+3. Notice that the second group of two beats doesn't have the bass drum; this is Kali, and it helps us identify where we are in the cycle. Recite the following syllables with the tabla recording.

Theka for Jhaptal

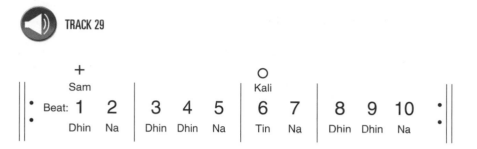

🔊 TRACK 29

COMPOSITION IN JHAPTAL

Notice again that the Gat ends on Sam (+).

Gat

🔊 TRACK 30

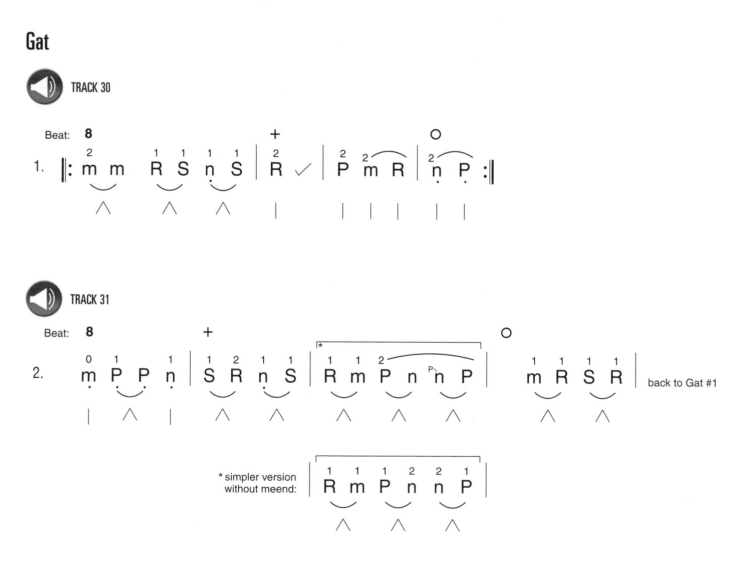

🔊 TRACK 31

Tans

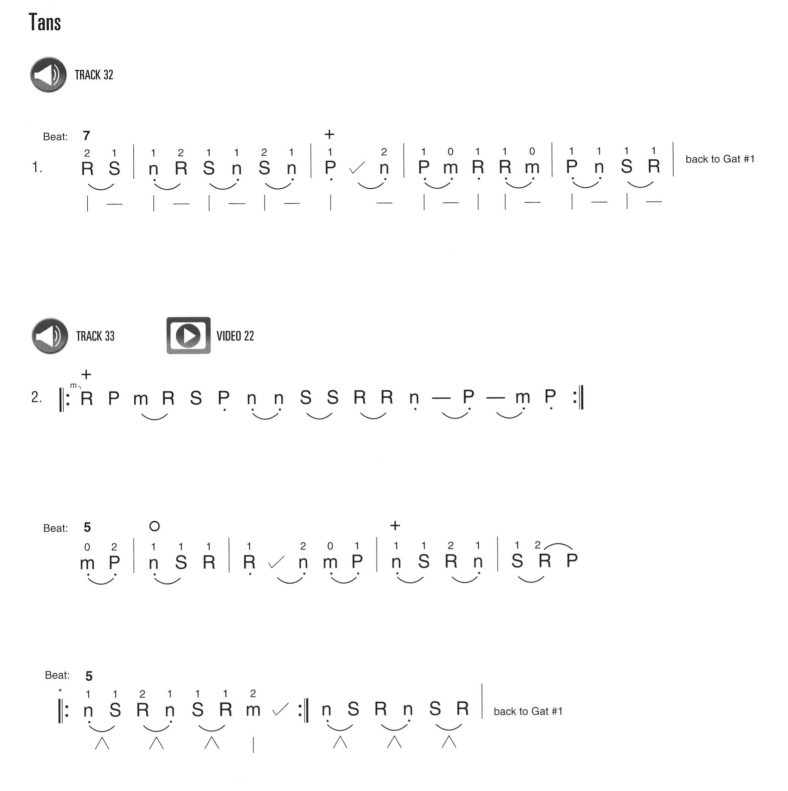

* Tihai: rhythm or phrase that repeats three times and lands
  on either Sam or the Mukhra (first line) of the Gat.

Antara

Antara is the second stage of a composition, emphasizing the upper range.

TRACK 34   VIDEO 23

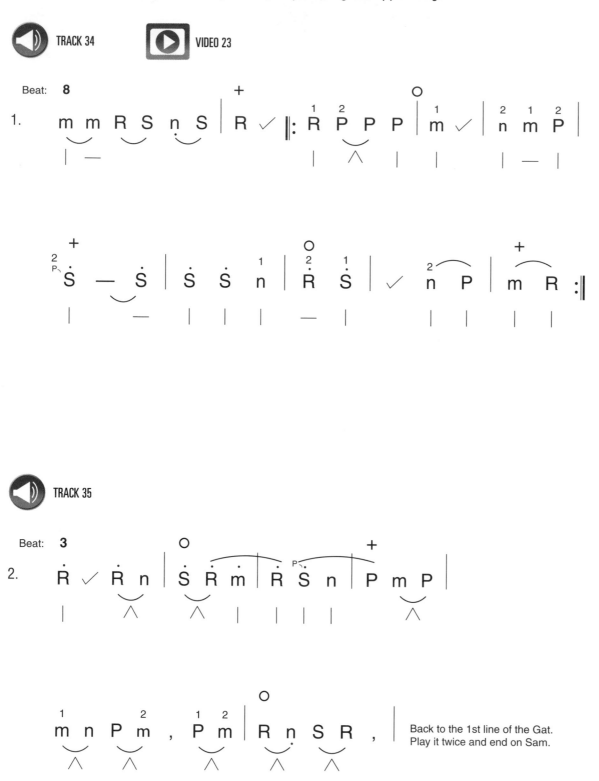

TRACK 35

Back to the 1st line of the Gat.
Play it twice and end on Sam.

KRINTAN

VIDEO 24

Krintan is the term we use for techniques that guitarists know as *hammer-ons*, *pull-offs*, and *slides*. These techniques are often intermingled with each other, as well as with bols and meend. This integration of techniques changes the tone and helps our music sound more interesting. Krintan requires a lot of strength and a sensitive touch to bring out each note clearly.

The following exercises are written in Bilawal, or the major scale. We will use krintan in the next composition in raag *Khammaj*. The scale for Khammaj is not exactly the same as Bilawal, but it is close enough for us to practice with Bilawal, and it is much more straightforward.

KRINTAN EXERCISES

The first type of krintan is a pull-off. For this technique, put your second finger on the low **Dha** (fret 4) and your index finger on the low **Pa** fret (fret 2). Pluck the **Dha**. While the note is sounding, pull the string sideways with the second finger of your left hand—the finger that is on the **Dha** fret. Don't just lift your finger off the string as you would normally do; you actually have to *pluck* the string to the side. You are basically plucking the string with your mizrab, and then plucking it again with your left middle finger in the opposite direction (mizrab up towards the ceiling, left middle finger down towards the floor). Practice the exercises slowly and deliberately before speeding them up.

TRACK 36

VIDEO 24
0:43

The next type of krintan is a hammer-on. For this technique, start with your first finger on the **Pa** fret. Now pluck the **Pa** and then hammer down onto the **Dha** with your second finger. You must do this with some force for the note to make a loud enough sound.

TRACK 36 (cont.)

VIDEO 24
2:32

Now let's combine the two types of krintan we just did. We'll play a hammer-on first and then a pull-off. This exercise contains three notes, but we're only going to pluck once on the first note. The other two are produced using the left hand.

TRACK 36 (cont.)

VIDEO 24
3:49

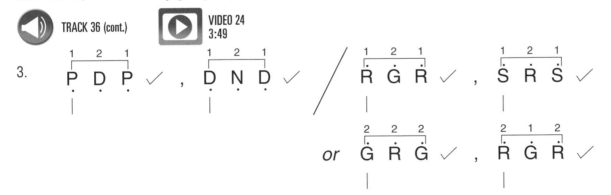

The last type of krintan is sliding. Start by putting your first finger on the low **Pa** fret. Now pluck, and while the note is sounding, slide your first finger up to **Dha**. Then pluck **Dha** and slide up to **Ni**, etc. Going down, we do the same thing in reverse. Keep in mind that the string has to be held firmly to the fret in order for the tone to continue. If you let the string come off the fret even for an instant, your finger will mute the string and the sound will die out. The trick here is to be firm while avoiding being tense.

TRACK 36 (cont.)

VIDEO 24
5:17

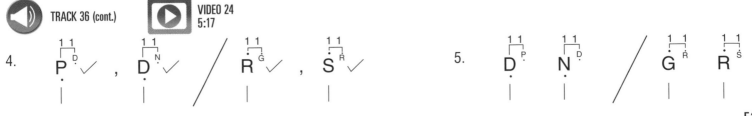

Now let's combine all the techniques.

6.
| 2   1   1   2   1   1   /   2   1   1   2   1   2
| N̤ Ḍ P. ✓ ,   S̤ N̤ Ḍ. ✓   /   G̣ Ṛ Ṡ. ✓ ,   Ṛ Ṡ̤ N. ✓
| | | |

7.
| 1   1   2   1   1   2   /   1   1   2   1   1   2
| P. Ḍ̤ N. ✓ ,   Ḍ. N̤ S. ✓   /   Ṡ̤ Ṛ̤ G̣ ✓ ,   N̤ Ṡ̤ Ṛ. ✓
| | | |

8.
| 1   1   2   1   1   1   2   1   /   1   1   2   1   1   1   2   1
| P. Ḍ̤ N̤ Ḍ. ✓ , Ḍ N̤ S̤ N̤. ✓   /   Ṡ. Ṛ̤ G̣̤ Ṛ̤ ✓ , N Ṡ̤ Ṛ̤ Ṡ̤ ✓
| | | |

9.
| 2   1   1   2   2   1   1   2   /   2   1   1   2   2   1   1   2
| N. Ḍ̤ P̤ Ḍ̤. ✓ , S N̤ Ḍ̤ N̤. ✓   /   G̣. Ṛ̤ Ṡ̤ Ṛ̤ ✓ , Ṛ. Ṡ̤ N̤ Ṡ̤ ✓
| | | |

10.
| 1   1   2   1   1   1   1   2   1   1   /   1   1   2   1   1   1   1   2   1   1
| P̤ Ḍ̤ N̤ Ḍ̤ P̤ , Ḍ̤ N̤ S̤ N̤ Ḍ̤   /   Ṡ̤ Ṛ̤ G̣ Ṛ̤ Ṡ̤ , N Ṡ̤ Ṛ̤ Ṡ̤ N
| | | |

11.
| 2   1   1   1   2   2   1   1   1   2   /   2   1   1   1   2   2   1   1   1   2
| N̤ Ḍ̤ P̤ Ḍ̤ N̤ , S̤ N̤ Ḍ̤ N̤ S̤   /   G̣ Ṛ̤ Ṡ̤ Ṛ̤ G̣ , Ṛ̤ Ṡ̤ N Ṡ̤ Ṛ̤
| | | |

 KHAMMAJ

Khammaj (Kha-mah-j) is an evening raga usually performed after sunset and before midnight. It is often played *mishra*, meaning "mixed." In a mishra performance, we can borrow notes or phrases from other ragas.

Khammaj is the main raga for *Khammaj That*, one of the ten main groups of scales. Khammaj That uses all the notes of the natural scale, plus komal **Ni** (flatted 7th).

TARAB TUNING

S Ṇ S R G m m P D n N Ṡ Ġ

SCALE

Khammaj That

S R G m P D n N Ṡ

ASCENDING AND DESCENDING SCALES

Aroha:

Ṇ S G m P D N Ṡ

Avaroha:

Ṡ n D P m G R S

RUPAK TAAL

Rupak Taal is a cycle of seven beats, grouped 3+2+2. Notice that Sam has no bass drum playing; this is also Kali. Rupak is the only taal in which Sam and Kali fall on the same beat. We show this by writing a plus sign inside a circle, as shown below.

Theka for Rupak Taal

TRACK 38   VIDEO 26 0:52

⊕						
1	2	3	4	5	6	7
Tin	Tin	Na	Dhin	na	Dhin	na

COMPOSITION IN RUPAK TAAL

This composition is set to medium-speed Rupak.

Gat

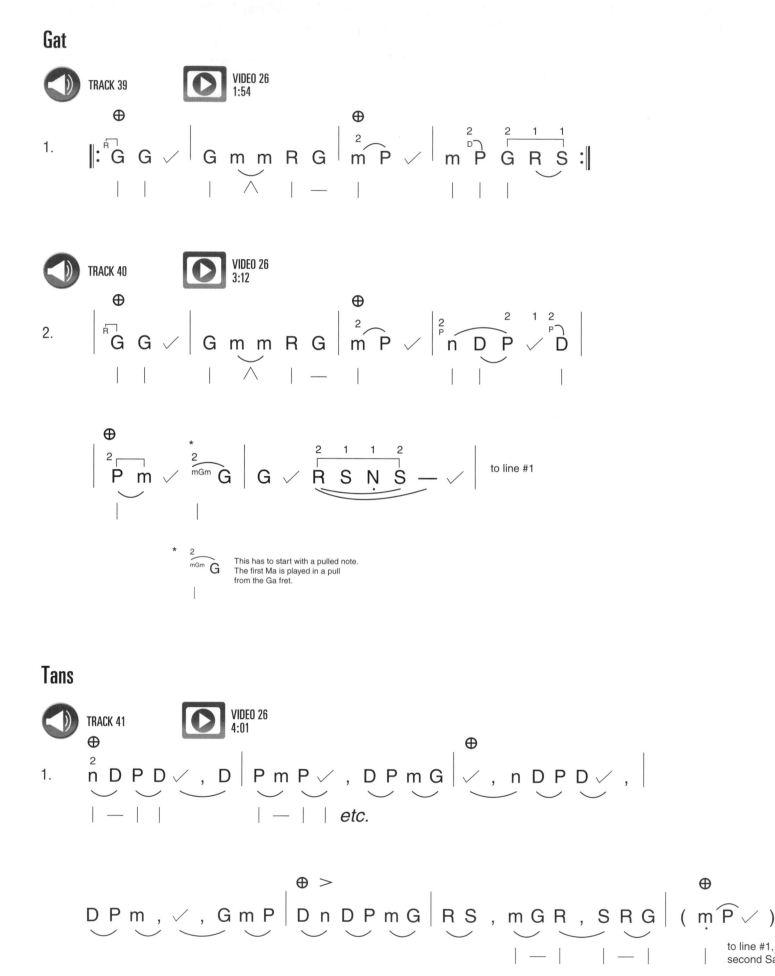

to line #1

* This has to start with a pulled note.
The first Ma is played in a pull
from the Ga fret.

Tans

etc.

to line #1,
second Sam

Notice that on the next example, the beat markings will only apply for the first time through a section. Refer to the recording.

TRACK 42   VIDEO 27

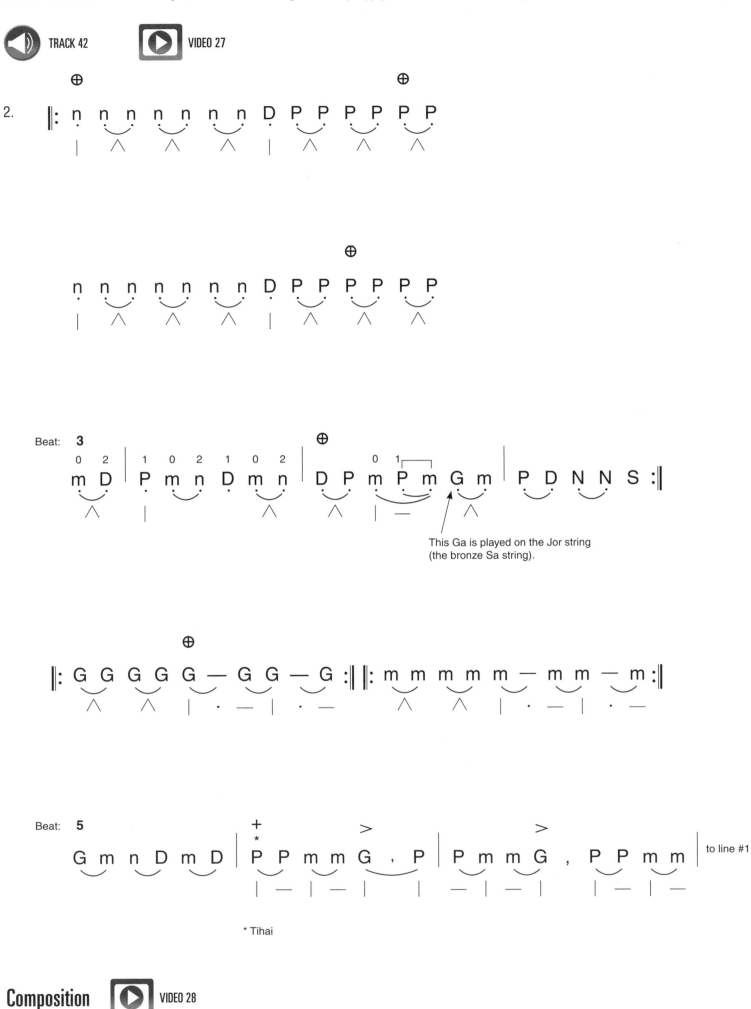

This Ga is played on the Jor string (the bronze Sa string).

* Tihai

Composition   VIDEO 28

APPENDIX

CHANGING STRINGS

Changing strings on the sitar can be a little tricky. If you want to be really good about it, you should change the main Ma string and the three chikari strings about every two or three weeks if you are practicing a lot. The sympathetic strings should be changed at least once a year, and the bronze strings should be changed two or three times a year at a minimum. The main issue with the strings is rust, bends from the frets, and metal fatigue, all of which lead to loss of quality tone and eventual breakage.

The photos shown here are for changing a sympathetic string, since there are more steps involved. The process for tying the string to the peg and tying the loop are the same for the main strings. **Change one string at a time!** That way you can check the other strings to make sure you are doing it properly.

Preferred String Gauges

Main		Chikari	
Ma	steel #3	Pa	steel #3
Sa	bronze #16	Sa	steel #1
Pa	bronze #22	Sa	steel #0
Low Sa	bronze #28		

Tarab (Sympathetic Strings)

steel #1 (many people prefer **steel #0**)

For tools, you will need a pair of needle nose pliers with wire cutters, music wire, and a big paperclip. You should pull open the paperclip so it is one long piece of metal, and then bend a hook about one half inch long on the tip.

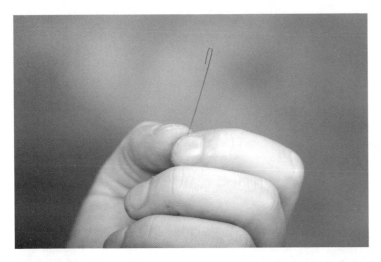

First, measure out your string. Your string should measure from the tail of the instrument to whatever peg you are going to tie it to, plus six inches. Once you cut it, you'll need to make a little hook at one end of the string.

Now insert the hook into the hole in the neck. You may need to use the pliers to help if it's not going in easily.

Next, take your paperclip and insert the hooked end into the peg hole in the neck. What you're trying to do here is to hook the paperclip around the hook on the string. Once you get it, pull the string out.

Now we have to tie the string to the tuning peg. If you can fit the hook on the string through the hole in the peg, then just push it through. If it won't go through, then cut the hook off, pass the string through the peg, and then make a new hook.

Take the long end of the string and go around the peg, so that when you go to put the peg back in the hole, the long end will be on top. Put the long end of the string *into* the hook.

Push the hook into the hole and pull the long end tight. Now the string is locked in; it will not slip and you shouldn't have a loose string end to scratch your sitar or cut you. Put the peg back into the hole now with the string attached.

For the other end of the string, make a loop with about one inch of string overlapping.

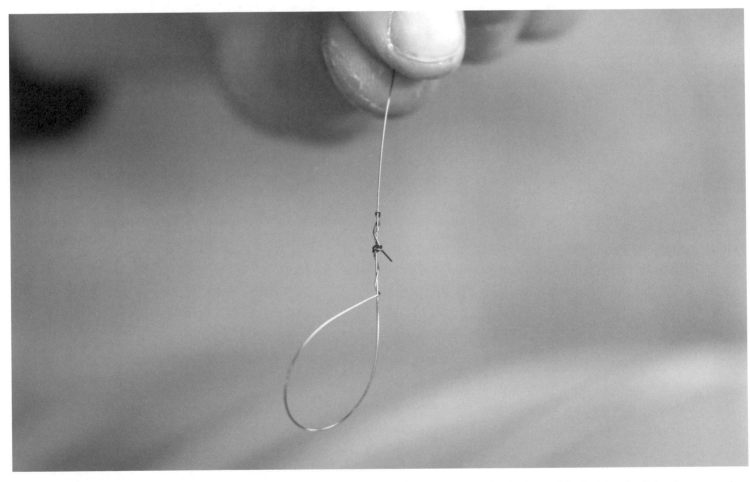

Now, twist the short end around the long part of the string. It's very important you try to keep this tight—don't let the wrapping spread out too much. Once you go around a few times, wrap it around a few more times going back over what you already did. This will lock it in so the wrapping doesn't come undone.

Pass the string under all the frets, over the small bridge, and under the big bridge. You'll want all the sympathetic strings to go through the same notch (in the middle) in the tailpiece. Once you get the loop to the end, put it around the post on the bottom of the instrument and hold it taut while you tighten the string using the peg. **Be careful not to hold the string too tightly!** If you pull too hard, you can bend the string permanently, and that will affect the tone.

GLOSSARY

accent: a note that is played louder, to give it emphasis.

Alap: the first portion of a performance when the raga is introduced without tabla. It is played rubato (not in fixed rhythm) and usually starts in the low register, moving up to the high register.

Alap-Jor-Jhalla: the full introduction of a raga, performed without tabla.

andolan: vibrato, or microtonal oscillation of a note.

Antara: the portion of a composition or melody that goes to the high Sa and above.

aroha: ascending, usually in reference to a scale.

avaroha: descending, usually in reference to a scale.

Bageshree: an evening raga usually performed between sundown and midnight.

bar line: a line used in notation that separates rhythmic groupings, or bars.

Bilawal Thaat: a scale in raga music that corresponds to the Western major scale.

bol: literally "word"; bols on sitar are right hand strokes.

chakradar: a type of tihai in which the tihai element is repeated three times. Therefore, a Chakradar contains nine repetitions. The final note of the last repetition will usually land either on Sam (beat 1), or before the Mukhra (beginning of the composition).

chalan: the way a raga moves. This may be straight up and down the scale, or may contain twists, turns, and pauses.

chikari: the drone/rhythm strings on the sitar.

comma: symbol used in notation to indicate phrasing.

Da, Ra, Diri, Chik: right hand plucks.
    Da: upstroke on the melody strings (dominant stroke).
    Ra: downstroke on the melody strings.
    Diri: Da Ra strokes played twice as fast.
    Chik: a downstroke on the chikari strings.

Dha, Na, Tin, Ge, Dhin: tabla strokes/notes.

gamak: a type of rapid oscillation or trill between two notes.

Gat: an instrumental composition that serves as a theme. Improvisations must always return to the Gat. The Gat may be repeated to mark the taal (rhythmic cycle) while the tabla player takes a solo.

grace note: an ornamental note that is usually shorter than the main note.

hammer-on: a left hand technique used to create a tone by hammering the string down onto the fret with enough force to make it vibrate.

jawari:
    1. the bridge of a sitar. There are two jawaris on the sitar: a larger one for the main strings, and a smaller one for the sympathetic strings.
    2. a term that describes the overtones/tone of an instrument or voice.
    3. the act of reshaping the bridge is referred to as "doing jawari."

Jhalla: the final portion of a performance usually characterized by fast right hand strokes and slow melodies. The main bol for Jhalla is Da Chik Chik Chik.

Jhaptal: a rhythmic cycle of 10 beats divided 2+3+2+3. Kali falls on beat 6. The theka is:
|| Dhin Na | Dhin Dhin Na | Tin Na | Dhin Dhin Na ||

Jor (form): the second section in the Alap. It is very similar to Alap and performed without tabla, however, it is performed with a steady, unmetered beat.

Jor (string): the second string on a sitar, tuned to Sa.

Kali: literally "black, empty"; the section of the rhythmic cycle in which the bass drum does not play resonant strokes. Every rhythmic cycle has Kali.

Kalyan Thaat: a scale in raga music corresponding to the Western Lydian scale/mode.

karaj: the low Sa string on a sitar.

Khammaj: an evening raga that is usually performed between sundown and midnight. It can be played in the classical or light classical style.

Khammaj That: a scale used in raga music. This scale is very similar to the Western major scale, but has both versions of the Ni (7th note). The shuddh Ni (natural 7th) is used ascending, and the komal Ni (flatted 7th) is used descending.

komal: literally "soft"; a note that is lowered one half step. Re, Ga, Dha, and Ni can be made komal. This term corresponds to the Western musical term "flat."

krintan: various left hand articulations that include hammer-ons, pull-offs, and slides.

Madhuvanti: a raga that originated in South India, but has been absorbed and performed in the North Indian style. Some people consider it a late afternoon raga, and some people consider it an evening raga. Madhuvanti uses a scale similar to Kalyan Thaat (Western Lydian scale/mode: major scale with a raised 4th note), but it also has the komal Ga (lowered 3rd note).

Malhar: a group of ragas associated with the monsoon or rainy season.

Malkauns: a late night raga that is usually performed from 12am to 3am. Malkauns has only five notes: Sa, komal Ga, Ma, komal Dha, and komal Ni.

meend: bending the notes/strings. On the sitar, this is done by pulling the string laterally across the frets. Meend is a very important part of raga music.

Megh: literally "cloud"; Megh is one of the main ragas of the Malhar group. It has only five notes: Sa, Re, Ma, Pa, and komal Ni.

mishra: literally "mixed"; a type of light classical performance in which the musician can introduce notes and phrases that are not native to the raga.

mizrab: the metal pick used to play sitar.

Mukhra: the first line of the Gat, leading up to Sam (beat 1). Mukh literally means "face."

murchhana: a type of melody pattern that spans a full octave.

octave: The interval between the first and eighth degrees of the Western diatonic scale.

palta: a pattern of notes that can be repeated successively up or down a scale.

pancham: literally "five"; the fifth note of a scale.

pentatonic: containing five notes.

pull-off: a type of left hand articulation that involves plucking the string with the left hand.

raga (raag): a melodic framework that is elaborated and improvised upon.

Rageshree: an evening raga usually played between sundown and midnight. It contains six notes: Sa, Re, Ga, Ma, Dha, and komal Ni.

repeat sign: a symbol used in notation that indicates to repeat particular sections of music.

rest: a period of silence in music.

rubato: freely slowing down and speeding up the tempo.

Rupak Taal: a rhythmic cycle of seven beats grouped 3+2+2. Kali falls on beat 1. The theka is:
|| Tin Tin Na | Dhin Na | Dhin Na ||

Sa, Re, Ga, Ma, Pa, Dha, Ni: the seven names assigned to the musical notes of sargam notation (the notational system of raga music). This corresponds to the Western solfege system. Sa and Pa cannot be altered. Re, Ga, Dha, and Ni can be played shuddh (natural) or komal (lowered a half step). Ma can be played shuddh (natural) or tivra (raised a half step).

Saath Sangat: a section of a performance when the melody instrument and the tabla player are both improvising/soloing at the same time. The tabla player will usually try to match the rhythm and phrasing of the melody in real time. Both players will try to come back to Sam (beat 1) together.

Sam: beat 1.

samvadi: the second most important note of a raga. It is almost always four or five notes away from the vadi (most important note). It is usually played more often and for longer durations than the other notes. Phrases will usually come to rest on either the vadi or samvadi.

sargam: the system of note names and notation in raga music.

Sargam composition: a type of vocal composition in which the note names are sung. These compositions are often used to aid learning, and are usually less complex than other types of composition.

Sawal Jawab: literally "question and answer"; a part of a performance when the melody instrument will state a phrase, and the tabla player will then echo it or reply to it with his own phrase of a similar length. It is usually done at the end of a performance at high speed. The melody instrument will usually start with longer phrases, and get progressively shorter as the section continues.

shruti: microtones, or notes in between the 12 half steps of an octave.

shuddh: a natural, unaltered note. A scale with all shuddh notes will correspond to the Western major scale.

slides: a type of left hand articulation in which a note is played with the index, middle, or ring finger of the left hand, and then moves, or slides, to another note without releasing the string.

slur: a type of notational symbol. It is an arcing line either above or below the notes.

solfege: a Western system of notation in which each of the seven notes of the major scale is given a name: Do, Re, Mi, Fa, Sol, La, Ti.

tabla: a drum mainly used in North India. The word tabla can refer to the pair of drums (tabla and baya) or just the right hand drum of the pair.

taal: literally "clap"; taal is the rhythmic side of raga music.

tanpura: the drone instrument used in raga music. Tanpuras can have four, five, or six strings.

tan: a fast line or run.

tarab: sympathetic strings. Also sometimes called "taraf."

theka: the specific strokes on the tabla that are associated with a rhythmic cycle (taal). They are fixed, however, the tabla player will usually use them as a base on which to elaborate or embellish.

tihai: a type of phrase in which a line is repeated three times. The last note of the third repetition will land either on Sam (beat 1) or the Mukhra (the first line of the composition).

Tintal: a rhythmic cycle of 16 beats grouped 4+4+4+4. Kali falls on beat 9. The theka is:

‖ Dha Dhin Dhin Dha ‖ Dha Dhin Dhin Dha ‖ Dha Tin Tin Na ‖ Na Dhin Dhin Dha ‖

tivra: a note that is raised a half step from natural. It corresponds to the Western musical term "sharp." The only note that can be made tivra is Ma.

tonal sequence: a melodic pattern that is repeated up or down a scale. This is done diatonically (only using notes within the scale).

toomba: gourd.

vadi: the most important note of a raga. It is usually played more often and for longer durations than the other notes. Phrases will usually come to rest on either the vadi or samvadi (second most important note).

Yaman: an evening melody usually performed between sundown and midnight. The scale corresponds to the Western Lydian scale/mode (a major scale with a raised 4th note).

Yaman Kalyan: an evening melody usually performed between sundown and midnight. It is very similar to raga Yaman, however some people make a distinction between the two by saying Yaman Kalyan contains the shuddh Ma (natural 4th note) in one phrase.

Learn To Play Today
with folk music instruction from

Hal Leonard Banjo Method – Second Edition

Authored by Mac Robertson, Robbie Clement & Will Schmid. This innovative method teaches 5-string, bluegrass style. The method consists of two instruction books and two cross-referenced supplement books that offer the beginner a carefully-paced and interest-keeping approach to the bluegrass style.

Method Book 1
00699500 Book $7.99
00695101 Book/CD Pack $16.99

Method Book 2
00699502..$7.99

Supplementary Songbooks
00699515 Easy Banjo Solos $9.99
00699516 More Easy Banjo Solos $9.99

Hal Leonard Dulcimer Method – Second Edition
by Neal Hellman

A beginning method for the Appalachian dulcimer with a unique new approach to solo melody and chord playing. Includes tuning, modes and many beautiful folk songs all demonstrated on the audio accompaniment. Music and tablature.
00699289 Book $8.99
00697230 Book/CD Pack $16.99

The Hal Leonard Complete Harmonica Method – Chromatic Harmonica
by Bobby Joe Holman

The only harmonica method to present the chromatic harmonica in 14 scales and modes in all 12 keys!
00841286 Book/Online Audio.............................$12.99

The Hal Leonard Complete Harmonica Method – The Diatonic Harmonica
by Bobby Joe Holman

This terrific method book/CD pack specific to the diatonic harmonica covers all six positions! It contains more than 20 songs and musical examples.
00841285 Book/CD Pack $12.95

Hal Leonard Fiddle Method
by Chris Wagoner

The Hal Leonard Fiddle Method is the perfect introduction to playing folk, bluegrass and country styles on the violin. Many traditional tunes are included to illustrate a variety of techniques. The accompanying audio includes many tracks for demonstration and play-along. Covers: instrument selection and care; playing positions; theory; slides & slurs; shuffle feel; bowing; drones; playing "backup"; cross-tuning; and much more!
00311415 Book $5.99
00311416 Book/Online Audio.............................$9.99

The Hal Leonard Mandolin Method – Second Edition

Noted mandolinist and teacher Rich Del Grosso has authored this excellent mandolin method that features great playable tunes in several styles (bluegrass, country, folk, blues) in standard music notation and tablature. The audio features play-along duets.
00699296 Book $7.99
00695102 Book/Online Audio $15.99

Hal Leonard Oud Method
by John Bilezikjian

This book teaches the fundamentals of standard Western music notation in the context of oud playing. It also covers: types of ouds, tuning the oud, playing position, how to string the oud, scales, chords, arpeggios, tremolo technique, studies and exercises, songs and rhythms from Armenia and the Middle East, and a CD with 25 tracks for demonstration and play along.
00695836 Book/CD Pack $12.99

Hal Leonard Ukulele Method Book 1
by Lil' Rev

INCLUDES TAB

This comprehensive and easy-to-use beginner's guide by acclaimed performer and uke master Lil' Rev includes many fun songs of different styles to learn and play. Includes: types of ukuleles, tuning, music reading, melody playing, chords, strumming, scales, tremolo, music notation and tablature, a variety of music styles, ukulele history and much more.
00695847 Book $6.99
00695832 Book/Online Audio.............................$10.99

HAL•LEONARD® CORPORATION
7777 W. BLUEMOUND RD. P.O. BOX 13819 MILWAUKEE, WI 53213

Visit Hal Leonard Online at
www.halleonard.com